Paul Rook
Co Founder / Co Owner

Paul Rook was born in Historic Greenwich, in December 1976, while the Christmas number one in the charts was 'A Child is born' he was raised in various areas of London and Kent. As he grew up he became involved with the cub scouts and learned various survival skills, which as time went on he was able to teach others in the scout movement. He also joined St John Ambulance at the age of 16 and assisted in setting up a St John Ambulance Cadet Unit. 25 years on He is still in the St John Ambulance and has risen to the skill set of Emergency Attendant.

As a young boy he loved all things paranormal and loved reading ghost stories and even telling some around the campfire when he was a scout. Having left that behind he got his first jobs working on the railways in Kent as a Cleaner working up to Fraud Officer, there were a lot of creepy stories of the paranormal surrounding many of the stations he visited which increased his passion for the paranormal.

He also briefly worked for the SOS Bus scheme in Southend-on-Sea and Basildon assisting in improving the policy for first aid treatments on the Bus. He also became a fully qualified First Responder with East of England Ambulance Service.

In 2016 Paul and other members of the SOS Bus received the Queens Award Medal for services to volunteering.

It all hasn't been smooth sailing for Paul Rook either, in 2016 due to some rivalry he was the victim of some malicious comments which took its toll and nearly destroyed everything Paul had worked for, He now suffers Depression and Anxiety and Panic attacks amongst other issues, So stamping out Bullying and making people aware of Mental Health within the paranormal field is something Paul has a deep passion for.

Like most teams out there these days, he used to watch paranormal related TV shows, and one day wondered, why don't I set up a team. It was a bit of fun at first but as his experiences grew so did his knowledge. This was when South Essex Paranormal was born, after 2 years though the team split up, and Paul never lost his passion or determination, but having learned by the mistakes he found 2 other business partners and set up a Paranormal Events Company that was called Trident Paranormal, this team lasted 4 years until one of the partners had to give up due to family problems, Paul thought this would be a perfect time to rebrand and refocus on his strengths, So now working under the banner of Phoenix he franchises out and has currently 3 teams over the UK which run the Paranormal Events, and on top of that Phoenix also caters for people who run events and need basic first aid cover. If you want to check Phoenix out for yourself then you can visit their website at www.phoenixevents.info

Then around 2014 he was invited to join an online radio podcast show that went out once a week where his passion heightened and he loved talking to new people in the field and formed some amazing friends and coworkers. When that podcast show ended in 2016 he joined forces with Richard Clements and together they started to grow Parasearch Radio into what it is today. Still learning and researching and meeting some amazing people along the way and sharing knowledge and helping others progress as much as possible. It hasn't been easy getting to where he is today within the Paranormal Community but with the help and support of his friends he has gone from strength to strength. Parasearch Radio

in 2019 was even nominated for the Higgypop Paranormal Awards in the category of Best Podcast which over the 3 years the station has been running is an amazing achievement.

Super humans
Written by Paul Rook

As many of you are all aware i have always been interested in the movies and comics, none so much as the Marvel and DC world movies and comics, from the mutants of The X Men to the Avengers right through to Batman and Suicide Squad, Humans with extra abilities have always fascinated me and this is why I chose much to Kerry's (my co host) disgust to do an entire show on Super humans.

I only knew of a few cases where one child in the US appeared to have superhuman strength, and a young Russian girl claimed to have X ray vision, I have vague recollections of those cases so thought I would dig up more, however what I found was so much more.

So it turns out that in order for the human race to evolve we need the mutant gene in every generation or we would never gain new skills. For example going back 12,000 years it was impossible for the average person to drink Cow's milk it wasn't until the human gene mutated that allowed us to progress to be able to drink Cow's milk and not get ill from it.

Scientists have concluded that when the human genome mutates and duplicates there are roughly 100 different mutations of that genome and its pretty common, so even if you could be a mutant right now and not even know about it. So it only stands to reason that every now and again someone in the face of adversity can and will stand up and use their superhuman ability and be noticed. They might not even know they have the super ability either.

Super Humans first appeared in the comic books around the 1930's with characters like The Phantom and Superman and Batman, and Children and Adults alike have been amazed with them ever since with new super humans coming out of the closet all the time.

In the Superhuman Show myself and Kerry talked about the different types of Superhuman abilities, such as those that people had self taught such as

Daniel Kish. He lost his sight as a child due to Cancer and he taught himself the ability of making small noises and listening to the sound coming back to him so he could map out his surroundings very much like a bat, he is dubbed the real Batman.

Others are mutations in the gene pool that give them special abilities such as Eero Mantyranta,
He was a Finnish Olympic Skiing Champion, and it's suggested that he was also the first sportsman to be tested positive for hormone doping , However it turns out that he along with members of his family had a rare mutation of the erythropoietin receptor gene, this allowed the carrier of this mutation to be able to carry 50% more oxygen in their bloodstream than people without the mutation, Something very useful for an athlete.

I also found details regarding people with amazing ability to remember every second of the day, we all know that long term and short term memory are stored in various parts of the brain, however research conducted by neuroscientists have agreed that both memory types are stored according to the activity of one particular gene in our body's, The gene is called the Rutabaga, and it is thought that it plays a major part in deciding where your memories are stored.

The first person to be diagnosed with this special memory power called Hyperaesthesia was a lady called Jill Price from Southern California. If you were to ask her what she had for dinner 25 years ago on any specific date she would be able to tell you in great detail and recall in great detail everything that happened then within a matter of seconds.

Jill was tested by medical staff to try to determine what caused her ability and Brain MRI scans could not shed any light on the subject, all that remains is DNA profiling however this has not been conducted.

On the show we covered so many more cases so if you want to learn more and see what other amazing abilities are out there, then your welcome to listen back to the podcast on the link below....

https://www.youtube.com/watch?v=ExU_b-0Br7Y

And please once you are listening feel free to subscribe to our channel.

The God Helmet.
Written by Paul Rook.

Myself and Kerry hosted a paranormal Concept show on The God Helmet, and we threw around some really interesting concepts that could have arisen from this piece of equipment, But I wanted to delve a little bit more into what The God Helmet was invented for and what it does and how its data can be used to make astounding claims, and can it scientifically backed up.

To give the God Helmet its true name The Koren Helmet, it was created by Stanley Koren who worked at Laurentian University as a Neuroscientist, Stanley Koren built upon the work of Dr M.R Persinger who designed the Helmet and Stanley built it using Persingers Specifications.

The whole concept was to study a person's creativity, religious experience and to see what effect the gentle stimulation had on the temporal lobe of the brain. The device is placed on the head of the willing volunteer and then wired up to an EEG machine, which studies the electrical impulses in the brains activities, The Helmet then emits a very weak electromagnetic field through the temporal lobes, which is quite painless and is no more powerful than a fridge magnet. Then the EEG records the results of brain activity.

However what we looked at in the show was that some of the people that were experimented on had very strange mystical experiences such as claiming to see images of God and / or Jesus.

In 2018 sometime before Persinger sadly passed away he was interviewed by a man called Tod Murphy and Tod asked the question, How many people have seen God using the Koren Helmet Persinger replied by saying :-
"The problem is producing an environment in which people will report what they experience without

anticipating ridicule on the one hand and not encouraging this type of report (demand characteristics) on the other.

Thus far, about 20 or so people have reported feeling the presence of Christ or even seeing him in the chamber (The acoustic chamber where the experimental sessions took place). Most of these people used Christ and God interchangeably. Most of these individuals were older (30 years or more) and religious (Roman Catholic). One male, age about 35 years old (alleged atheist but early childhood RC (Roman Catholic) training), saw a clear apparition (shoulders and head) of Christ staring him in the face. He was quite "shaken" by the experience. I did not complete a follow-up re: his change in behaviour. Of course these are all reports. What we did find with one world-class psychic who experiences Christ as a component of his abilities was we could experimentally increase or decrease his numbers of his reported experiences by applying the LTP pattern (derived from the hippocampus) over the right hemisphere (without his awareness).

The field on-response delay was about 10 to 20 sec. The optimal pattern, at least for this person, looked very right hippocampus. By far most presences are attributed to dead relatives, the Great Forces, a spirit, or something equivalent.

The attribution towards along a devil to angel continuum appears strongly related to the affect (pleasant-terror) associated with the experience. I suspect most people would call the "vague, all-around-me" sensations "God" but they are reluctant to employ the label in a laboratory. The implicit is obvious. If the equipment and the experiment produced the presence that was God, then the extra personal, unreachable and independent characteristics of the god definition might be challenged."

*The below quotation was found and taken from http://www.innerworlds.50megs.com/God_Helmet/god_helmet.htm

The God and religious experience i feel was an unexpected outcome to what Persinger wanted to study as he wanted to test out a few of his theories about how the brain works and that the 2 halves of the brain work together instead of having a dominant and dormant side.

Myself and Kerry went delving into a lot of other theories about frequencies and vibrations resulting from this work, but I do think it can stimulate the brain into so much more not only religious visitations but spiritual as well. as some of what was reported is indicative of outer body experiences, and astral projection and not forgetting the emotions it could also illicit.

This could also raise the question of manifestations in paranormal activity, could our brains be working on certain frequencies that could manifest a vision that we perceive as spirit while on investigations if our emotions are running high ?

Or could it be that the spirits and spirit world is manifested from within especially if you have a belief system in place ?

In the show we went down so many rabbit holes with this concept and bounced around loads of ideas so if you would like to learn more then please listen to the podcast. (Link Below)

Also feel free to comment as we would love to hear your ideas and views on The Koren Helmet AKA The God Helmet.
https://www.spreaker.com/user/parasearchuk/paranormal-concept-persingers-helmet

Animal Spirits
Written by Paul Rook

For centuries and for as long as man has gazed up at the stars animals have been a part of religion and theology.

Animals have played a huge part in human evolution, and some have even got the intelligence to work with and alongside us to, so this makes them just as important as the human race.

We have done shows before on the origins of Animal Spirits Guides and their meaning, but we wanted to discuss something different this time. We did although touch on some of the ancients aspects of Animal spirits and how they become to be someone's spirit guide, and of course discussed the rainbow bridge concept. But we wondered do Animals actually haunt locations ?

Firstly we looked at the intelligent level of an animal, is this something that gives the animal a sense of self aware so much that it can literally haunt a location ? Or do animals have the power to self manifest spirit in the same way it is theorised that humans can ?

We also discussed the animal instinct and the relationship between animal and human, does that bond somehow carry over to the spirit world and allow the animal spirits to return ? I believe it does, and it has been reported so many times that animal owners can still feel and hear their deceased pets.
We even discussed a few theories as to why we don't really get to see any spirits of Dinosaurs, and the possibility of capturing evidence of animal spirits at The Tower of London. The Tower of London was basically the origins of London Zoo, and great discoverers of the world would bring back newly discovered

animals for the crown and keep them outside of the Tower of London for the public to see. So would Spirits of Animals still be there to this day, It's hard to say with the noise pollution and constant lights etc...

We also touched upon reports of spirit animals from across the world from Elephants, Tigers and the infamous Black Shuck, and how stories and legends can spread across the world.

Just an afterthought but could even reports of BigFoot and the Loch Ness Monster type creatures even be spirits of animals from the past ? Who is to know...I do think that Animal Spirits should be looked into a lot more as the subject and myths and legends that surround the animal kingdom is gigantic, and is very ell tied in and linked to human society. We can still learn a lot from animals. It would be interesting to see how we could learn from them in the Paranormal field as we know that animals such as cats and dogs are open to alleged spirits, Cats were even used to ward off evil spirits, this is why so many old houses were made and cats were bricked up in the walls.

For a chance to learn more about what we discussed and the theories we stumbled upon please have a listen to The Paranormal Concept Show. The link is below. Also please feel free to comment as we like to hear what you think.

https://www.spreaker.com/user/parasearchuk/paranormal-concept-show-spirit-animals

Time Travel in the movies.
Written by Paul Rook.

I Have thought long and hard on how to approach the subject of Time Travel,
so much that, as you all know im influenced and interested in the movies i thought this would be a perfect way for me to talk about Time Travel.

For a long time now scientists have always theorised that Time Travel forward in time is possible, by travelling as close as they can to the speed of light. The closer to the speed of light you travel the slower time moves for you, and slower for the rest of us, so what would be a 10 minute journey for you at high speed would indeed be years for us at regular speed. Now let's take a look at travelling backwards in time H.G. Wells style with his immortal classic "Time Machine". In this story the main character's Wife/

Girlfriend gets murdered so he sets about inventing a time machine to alter history so that she survives.

This however does not pan out as every time he goes back she dies from something else like its a fixed point in time so she is destined to die. That is one theory so no matter what you do you can not change history. However that said let's look at the way the time machine worked, In the movie remake the machine created a bubble around the machine and as you look out of the bubble you can see time rewinding or fast forwarding depending as to whether going forward and backwards in time, So the capsule is static and the world is moving around it, This wouldn't work as the Earth and Solar System is also moving so if the capsule is static not only would you see time rewinding and fast forwarding but you would also see the planet and solar system spiralling away from you. So i think that is a flaw in the Time Machine.

I also want to say out of all the Time Travel movies and TV Shows, I actually believe that Dr Who has got Time Travel mastered !

The Tardis which stands for Time And relative Dimensions In Space, travels 3 different ways, When travelling through time it travels through the time vortex and drops out when its reached its desired time and then lands on whatever planet The Doctor happens to visit.

When The Doctor wants to travel from one point to another on the same planet the TARDIS phases from point A to point B although if The Doctor wanted to he could also fly The TARDIS as you would a plane (Like in the episode 'The Runaway Bride'. The TARDIS has to be one of the most well thought out Time Machines of the 20th Century. Well done the BBC for that !

Next I want to look at Back to the future...This movie story gets quite complicated, as the main character "Marty" travels from 1985 to 1955 meets his parents and interferes with time, then gets back to 1985 only for his friend "The Doc" to come back and take him to 2016 to save his future son from prison, and someone steals the time machine and alters the past, creating an alternate reality that the doc and Marty travel back in time to 1985 only to go back to return the timeline back in 1955 before the doc gets zapped back to 1855 ....Hope you got all that.

Oh dear where to begin with the flaws in this movie....lol, Let's look at the way the time machine works again its a static machine although it takes into consideration the date and time it does not specify a location so there for it has the same issue as H.G.Wells's time machine, in the respect that the time machine would end up most of its life in space (well until its conversion to Hover Car in 2015) and also despite the fact that the time machine car needs to reach a speed of 88 MPH although if the machine creates a vortex to travel too at the point of spontaneous transference then that cold be an explanation as to how it works although that is not something covered in the movie.

I have also come to the conclusion that Back to the Future is a pointless movie, because when Marty travelled back in time he interfered with his mum meeting his dad, thus the film is basically trying to get the timeline reverted back so that Marty was not erased from the future which obviously he was successful at. However if after interfering Marty did nothing then Marty would of been erased from the timeline, and as future Marty does not exist any more he wouldn't be able to come back to interfere so there for the timeline would have reverted back to what it should of been. So this got me thinking would changing the past actually work ?

Personally I believe it wouldn't and here is why.... Let's say you decided to climb into your time machine on your 20th birthday and kill Hitler at birth, by making that change you could in fact create a butterfly effect through time and create a new timeline with Hitler not in it as you wished, now if you then went back to your own timeline (If you could) that version of you would cease to exist and hopefully as the new timeline plays out and your lucky enough to have the new version of you were born, you would not know who Hitler was so would have no desire to protect the existing timeline by getting to your 20th Birthday to travel back in time to kill Hitler at birth, thus the timeline would then revert back to the original timeline.

Complicated I know hence why its taken this long to write this blog.

because of this theory, I have concluded that it could be possible that the cosmos in its infinite wisdom has safeguarded itself from any one attempting to alter the past because we all have a purpose and are destined for whatever reason.

Now going into Mark Manleys territory for a while....even if we could travel back in time just to observe we would have an effect on history, now assuming that reports of UFO's through the thousands of years are genuine, could they be time travel crafts and only here to observe, and by appearing in our skies they have influenced us to wonder at the stars and make the technology to reach them, so we are of our own creation. Not to mention the religious interpretations across the globe.

Life of a Presenter !
Written by Paul Rook

One thing I love about being a Parasearch Presenter is the different people I get to talk to in the field of the Paranormal and from all walks of life, about something we all share a passion in. But being a presenter isn't just about putting out a show for an hour a week, there is so much more to do behind the scenes.

Yes we do put out a show for an hour once a week providing Kerry don't twist our arms to put out a pop up show lol but we also like to plan 4 weeks in advance, so that includes trawling through various social media to find out the latest in the world of the paranormal for subjects, then we would like to see if we can find volunteers to join us on air to give you our listeners the best and updated information....

And if that isn't enough, we also have to surprisingly do some research, because as much as we are learning from the guest and talking to them we do need to have a slight understanding of the subject to be able to have a conversation with someone about it, this too is something I love to do, i love to learn and to also talk to someone in that area of expertise (for the want of a better word) is amazing and we can learn so much from them,

particularly the older generation of investigator, they have been in the field a lot longer than most people listening and they have so much information to pass on its unbelievable, if we have one of the older generation on our shows you can bet once the show finishes and goes off air we are still talking to them over skype and learning more and getting more ideas for new shows to bring you even more information.

Although we do provide our listeners with as much information as possible we do like to keep the conversations light and relaxed so its more comfortable for you to listen and the conversation to flow and make everyone feel at ease and with the live chat room it brings everyone together in a much more friendly environment as we feel the Paranormal World should be.

So once we have decided the topic, Secured the Guests, Raised the Event, Researched the show subject, Put out the show......We start all over again for the following week !....Who would be a Presenter ?? Must be mad....Its a full time job sometimes but that said I love to do it. On top of that we don't get paid for it either. But it's a passion so i don't mind at all and neither do any of the other presenters.

We are always looking for new ideas, subjects, competition prizes & Guests so if you have something to offer and want to be a part of Parasearch Family then please contact us via our online form that you can find at www.parasearch.org (It would make my life easier lol)

For most of the presenters we also hold day jobs or/and also Paranormal Investigators ourselves with teams to run....anyone would think we live and breath Paranormal and don't like to have free time....but we manage just because it's our passion and we like to share our knowledge base with you all, and we enjoy talking to you all even if it is through a chatroom, who knows maybe you will one day be on one of our shows.

The Hidden Castle
Written by Paul Rook.

On the 10th August 2019, Richard Clements and I visited a little known gem of a castle known by the locals as 'The Hidden Castle' but to the rest of the country it is known as New Buckenham Castle. It is based just on the outside of the small village of New Buckenham deep in the Norfolk countryside. The village was founded between 1146 & 1176 by a man called William D'Albini.

The village was designed as a typical Normal settlement, and still to this day remains the same layout.

The village was created just to the east of just new castle. The village was situated close to another village called Old Buckenham. The village has a rich and full medieval history which is documented and kept in the old parish records office.

The following Extract is taken from :-
www.heritage.norfolk.gov.uk

The earlier history of the landscape is less well known. The earliest find recorded in the database is a Neolithic axehead . Several other undated prehistoric worked flints have also been found. Traces of Bronze Age barrows were recorded in the 19th century on Buckenham Common but no trace of them can be seen now. The site of two possible Bronze Age barrows was recorded in the 19th century but the mounds are no longer there. Prehistoric pot has also been recorded. Field walking in part of New Buckenham Castle's south-west bailey just outside the parish boundary recovered pieces of Iron Age pot.

New Buckenham Castle is actually in Old Buckenham parish but for the sake of completeness will be described here. The D'Albini established this substantial castle around 1146 to replace Old

Buckenham Castle. The circular ring work of New Buckenham Castle contains the oldest, and perhaps the largest, circular Norman keep in the country.

The castle has two baileys. The east bailey (recorded as Knight riders Ward in an old document) is the earliest. It was reached via an east gateway that was destroyed in the 13th century when the bank of the ring work was enlarged almost burying the gatehouse. A second bailey, gatehouse and barbican-like defensive enclosure were then constructed to the south-west. The castle was besieged twice in the 13th and 15th centuries. It was de fortified in the 1640s. St Mary's Chapel is adjacent to the castle. William D'Albini founded this in the 12th century to serve the parishioners of his planned town and the inhabitants of his castle. At some stage in its history it was served by the canons of St James' Priory.

When the parish church of St Martin was built in New Buckenham in the 13th century the chapel became the private chapel of the castle. At some time in the 15th century large traceries windows were inserted. The chapel appears to have survived the Reformation, perhaps continuing in use until the de fortification of the castle in 1649. The castle and chapel were surrounded by Buckenham deer park that was laid out around 1100 to surround Old Buckenham Castle. D'Albini's son, William the Strong, expanded the park in the 12th century probably as part of his development of New Buckenham Castle and the planned town

I also want to share this extract from :- www.britainexpress.com
William d'Albini was one of the Norman barons who supported William the Conqueror in his conquest of England in 1066. In gratitude for his support William gave d'Albini vast estates in Norfolk. D'Albini built Castle Rising, near King's Lynn, and to defend his estates in south Norfolk he built a castle at Buckenham, a Saxon settlement south of Attleborough.

In 1145 d'Albini son, also named William, gave the Buckenham castle to the Augustinian order of canons to help found a new priory, and he began to build a much larger and more ambitious moated fortress a short distance to the south-east. The new location was better situated, on the main road between Thetford and Norwich.

The Augustinian s were granted the old castle site on condition that they destroy the defences to prevent them being used by the king's enemies. The canons used the building materials of the old castle to create Old Buckenham Priory. The only part of the priory still standing today is a section of the monastic church.

To service his new castle d'Albini built a planned town, named New Buckenham to distinguish it from the older Saxon settlement. New Buckenham is the only village in England to retain its original street layout. The village was laid out on a regular grid pattern, bounded by its own defensive earthwork wall and ditch. To supply produce for the castle the village was granted a charter to hold a market, a valuable right in those days.

New Buckenham grew wealthy on the proceeds of the tanning industry, and inside the earthworks they built fine timber-framed buildings. Most of the historic buildings still survive, though many are now hidden behind later Victorian facades. Outside the earthworks is New Buckenham Common, one of the largest commons in the country.

As for the d'Albini new castle, it was protected by an almost perfectly circular moat, enclosing two outer Baileys and an inner bailey. Within the inner bailey was the heart of the castle, a circular stone keep said to be the earliest in England. The keep had massive walls, up to 11 feet thick at the base, and rising to 40 feet high. The keep is built of local flint.

It must have been an extraordinary fortress by the time it was finished in 1176, a statement of the d'Albini's power and influence. As a point of curiosity the castle is actually in Old Buckenham Parish, but has always been called New Buckenham Castle.

And it needed to be strong, for the d'Albini's fell from grace under King John, who, to be fair, was at odds with almost everyone. The d'Albini's initially supported King John in his struggle with the barons that led to the Magna Carta, but they eventually deserted the king and joined his enemies. In response the king razed the d'Albini lands, but it isn't certain that he actually attacked the castle at New Buckenham.

Rebellious against one king, the d'Albinis stayed loyal to Henry III during Simon de Montfort's Baron's War in 1263. Sir Henry de Hastyngs, a supporter of de Montfort, attacked the castle but was repulsed. He had to content himself with ravaging the countryside.

By 1461 the castle was owned by Sir John Knyvet, a Lancastrian supporter in the Wars of the Roses. The Yorkist King Edward IV sent troops to subdue the castle but they were beaten back by loyal soldiers led by Sir John's wife Alice. According to reports at the time Alice Knyvet stood atop the castle keep and shouted to the enemy that she would die defending the castle. She had no need to, for the king's men retreated.

Inside the outer bailey wall stood a chapel, dedicated to St Mary. William d'Albini established the chapel to serve the parishioners of his newly planned town. It was served briefly by St James Priory. When the new parish church of St Martin was erected in the 13th century the chapel became a private chapel for the castle residents. The chapel fell out of use during the Dissolution of the Monasteries and was used as a cattle barn.

The medieval fortress was in poor condition by the time of the Civil War. The owner was Sir Philip Knyvet, who paid lip service to Parliamentary support. In 1649 Parliament ordered the castle destroyed, fearing that it might be seized by Royalist supporters and held against them.

As a result, only the lower sections of the keep walls remain, with a few other crumbling sections of wall and the remains of the outer gatehouse. The impressive earth ramparts remain, however, soaring 40 feet above the moat. The earthworks are overwhelmed with trees and undergrowth, but you can climb a set of steps to the top of the rampart.

It is also rumoured that a local legend says that the castle was where the Gunpowder Plot of 1605 was hatched.

I do not want to take any credit for writing this Blog as 95% of it was taken from other people's research but I have cited the links to their work so they are the ones to credit for this work.

I just stumbled across this little gem and I wanted to share it with you all. So if you get a chance to visit this location one day then do it.

The Mysterious Green Children of Woolpit.
Written by Paul Rook

For a few years now I have been fascinated by the Folklore legend regarding the Green Children and the village of Wolfpit, or Woolpit as it is now known.

This was regarding an incident that was documented by two, twelfth century Chronicle writers. one being Ralph of Coggeshall an Abbot of a Cistercian Monastery at Coggeshall, and William of Newburgh who was an English Historian and Cannon at the Augustinian Priory in North Yorkshire.

William claimed the legend began back in the reign of King Stephen (1135 - 1154 AD), where the Ralph wrote his chronicles between 1187 till 1224 and he was known to travel around the East Anglia region of the UK where he picked up a lot of information to document. he claimed the children were found during the reign of Henry II, depending on who's document you read. For the sake of this Blog, I am looking at the document written by William of Newburgh.

There was a 3rd person who documented this although he just published the story in a document called 'Otia Imperialia' which told of all the known legends in England at the time, His name was Gervase of Tilbury, he was born in Tilbury Essex and became the Marshal of the Kingdom on the Arles under the Emperor Otto IV. It is widely debated on which document he took the legend from. It will be one of those things we will never know.

The legend states that in the 12th century at the Parish of St Mary of Woolpit in Suffolk, A boy was discovered along with his sister by some local peasants at the edge of a Wolf Pit. They looked like other people but with one difference, the colour of their skin. It was tinged with a green colour, not only this but no one could understand their language.

Everyone was amazed, as the children wept inconsolably, as they were taken to a house near Wikes, it was the home of Richard De Calne's where they were offered lots of food but they just would not eat, For a long tie they suffered hunger, because as the girl told someone later they thought the food was inedible. The only thing they ate was Peas, One of the villagers brought in some peas and the children got very excited and literally snatched the peas to eat, They would not touch any other food other than the peas for a long time afterwards.

The boy always appeared to be tired and of ill health and sadly died a short time afterwards, however the girl survived and grew accustomed to an array of foods and liked them. As she grew she also lost the green tinge completely and regained a normal pink colour. She was also baptized and admitted into the Christian Church. It was reported she lived with a Knight and his family for many years although remained too playful and wilful.

And here is the interesting part ....

the girl was questioned about her people of her country. She declared that all inhabitants and everything, which existed in that country was tinged with a greenish colour, and that they saw no sun, and they only had a small amount of light rather like an afterglow at sunset. She was also asked how she and her brother had reached this land. She replied that it happened when they were following their flocks and they discovered a cave, and upon entering they could hear bells.

They were captivated by the sound and ventured deeper into the cave. they were going for a long while until they came to the mouth of the cave system and was dazzled by the brilliance of sunlight and the warmth that they have never experienced and stayed there for a while, When the villagers found the children they were frightened and wanted to run away but could not find the entrance back into the cave.

When myself and Richard visited Woolpit, we happened upon a small museum in the village and we purchased a booklet on this subject by Elizabeth Cockayne. In the booklet it offers an explanation as to the legend of the Green Children, The next part of the blog is quoted directly from the booklet.

'In the latter half of the 12th century Robert De Bermont, the Duke of Leicester quarreled with, Henry II. In 1173 he landed on the coast of Suffolk with a force of Flemish mercenaries, with a view to deposing Henry. The Duke's men were massacred on the banks of the river Lark at Fornham St Genevieve, which is the village adjacent to Fornham St. Martin, By the King's army. The Duke and his wife were taken prisoner.

Of the camp followers there is no report. However, it is possible that among them were children and it is possible that two escaped and fled into the countryside. To survive they would of had to eat leaves and berries from the bushes, and at night would huddle together.
As their diet lacked any red meat or other iron rich based foods they would soon become anaemic, giving rise to the medical condition known as Chlorosis, or

the green sickness, which would cause the skin to take on a green tinge.

After wandering for several months they could have fallen into an old overgrown clay pit on the Woolpit/Elmswood border. It is known that the Romans dug clay pits in the area. This was where the villagers of Woolpit found the children. Alone, Frightened and disorientated. Had they been stunned by their fall ? In this confused state no wonder they did not respond to the torrent of questions put to them. Certainly if they were Flemish, they would not have understood the Suffolk labourers.

The villagers would have been equally baffled, until someone suggested taking them to the nearest speaker of a foreign tongue, namely Sir Richard De Calne of Wykes Hall, (thought to be Wyken Hall near Bardwell), who would have certainly spoken French.
Once at Wyken Hall, although unable to understand them, Sir Richard offered them a home. The boy, the youngest one of the two was obviously quite ill; he grew weaker and died soon after, but the girl survived

and began to eat a normal diet, and her skin soon lost the green tinge.

She learned to speak English, and claimed they had come from the land of St Martin, which was in perpetual twilight, from which they could see a sunny land across the big river. Was this Fornham St Martin which is just across the river Lark from Fornham St Genevieve? They are only two or three miles away from Bury St Edmunds.

If the children had only recently arrived from the continent everything would be very strange to them, they would speak in a completely different language. The bells of the abbey of St Edmund could be heard from the Fornhams, which would account for the hearing of the bells.

The story goes on to say that the girl married a man from Lynn (Known as Kings lynn.)'

My thoughts on this legend.

I actually like the explanation given in the booklet and can buy most of it however I do have a few other theories as to why the children were described as having green skin.

As already stated it could have been a medical condition brought on by the children's diet.

However I have been wondering lately if it has another meaning and lost in translation.

When describing the children as lost and frightened could they also appeared to be as we describe people now as green skinned meaning innocent and naive ?

Another theory I've also tried to look into without too much success is that hundreds of years ago, we didn't have a word for blue, instead it was quite common to say the word Green as a shade of Blue, so i think it would be possible for the children to be blue with cold, and because we had no word for Blue they were described as Green. I am not sure of when this would come about in the English Language but it's certainly a fact, and could be another reason the children were described as Green.

To be honest we will never know, but if your like me you will be intrigued for ever more.

The Black Shuck : Origins
Written by Paul Rook.

Firstly, for those that do not know what a Black Shuck is, It's an Urban Legend that is supposedly witnessed in and around coastal areas of East Anglia.

The Black Shuck has mainly been described as a big black long haired dog with piercing Red Glowing Eyes. However depending on where you go in East Anglia, the description does slightly vary. (See the Picture to the Right) It is said that the Black Shuck haunts the Footpaths, Lanes, Churchyards, Crossroads & Pre Historic Sites. around the coast of East Anglia. They are also thought to be haunting areas where the veil between realms are thinnest, and are also suggested to be found between or on ley lines.

No one really knows when the legend of the Black Shuck really started although there are a few stories around.

Looking into the origins of the Black Shuck there is a claim that in Norse Mythology The Black Shuck is really the companion of Thor God of Thunder called Shukir and that the Shuck accompanied Thor to the English shore.

It is suggested that the Shuck was the god of war, although looking into this theory I have found that, although pets were rife within Norse mythology, however there is no mention at all anywhere that Odin or Thor had a dog. The closest I could find is that Odin had 2 wolves called Geri and Freki, both wolves followed Odin into battle but they didn't really play a major part in the mythology just like Odin's Ravens. As for Thor, he is not mentioned to have any association with any animal other than Goats that pulled his chariot. There is a mention in Norse Mythology that there are 2 dogs or Hell Hounds that guard the gates of Hell and some believe that this could also account for the Black Shuck sightings however i very much doubt it and think it can be a very loose connection.

Now leaving the most interesting Norse Mythology behind, there is another story which involves the premise that the Black Shuck is a spirit. It is said that one fateful night, 2 friends, one a Saxon fisherman and a Danish fisherman and their dog, went on a late night fishing trip into the north sea / English Channel and they got into difficulties and the fishing boat sank, the body of the Danish man was washed up in Overstrand and the Saxon man washed up in Beeston.

The body of their dog was never found, however its suggested that the spirit of their dog was left wondering the East Anglia Coast in search of his poor masters. This story again assuming spirits do exist is probably the more logical (although not saying they do) , however I can not substantiate the claim as without more exact details of names and a year it's hard to pinpoint if this incident actually happened. But looking into the newspaper reports Beeston does have a history of having bodies found on its beaches. So it's not in the realms of impossibility.

There is also a lot of dubious Occult origins of the Black Shuck claiming that the Devil had been summoned up from Hell and changed form and for anyone that is unlucky enough to witness the Black Shuck they are allegedly plagued with misfortune. But I for one do not think for one second that this is the case, and this Blog is not to debate the existence of the Devil whatever form he/she may take.

I have also found other Black Dog stories from all over the UK including Scotland where it is suggested that Black Dogs are imagined to be protectors of treasures, could there be a truth in this because as we know already there has been a rise in uncovering treasure troves in the UK particularly in the East Anglia region.

So could there be a truth in this Scottish myth ? if indeed it is a Myth.

One of the first of the legends to arise with the Black Shuck is as follows. I took this statement from www.thesuffolkcoast.co.uk

"On 4th August 1577, a large black dog burst in through the doors of St Mary's Church in Bungay to a clap of thunder. It ran up the nave, past a large congregation, killing a man and boy and causing the church steeple to collapse through the roof, before moving on to Blythburgh Church where it mauled and killed more people.

Local accounts attribute the event to the Devil - The scorch marks on the door of Blythburgh Church are referred to by the locals as "the devil's fingerprints" which can be seen at the church to this day.

The spine-chilling event is remembered in this verse:

"All down the church in the midst of fire, the hellish monster flew, and, passing onward to the quire, he many people slew".

According to folklore, the 'Bungay Black Dog' prowls along dark lanes and lonesome field footpaths of The

Suffolk Coast, where, although his howling makes the hearer's blood run cold, his footfalls make no sound. If you are unfortunate enough to encounter him it is said that you will soon be extremely ill-fated!

Today, you can see evidence of the mythical creature; the scorch marks on the door at Blythburgh church and throughout the market town of Bungay."

Both myself and Richard yet have to hold a Road Trip to Bungay, but it is definitely on the list of places to visit, We will find the church and conduct a live feed from there so we can show you the evidence to go with the story, However is it proof of the black Shuck or is it something else. If you are interested in watching the LIVE feed when we visit Bungay please visit our wonderful Facebook group Parasearch Radio Group page at https://www.facebook.com/groups/parasearch/

This is something that we will probably never know, but certainly an interesting cryptozoological / Paranormal case whatever you believe.

The Black Shuck : Legends
Written by Paul Rook.

To follow on from the Blog I wrote regarding The Black Shuck Origins, particularly around the East Anglia Coast, I thought I would write a follow up with some of the other sightings from around the UK, as it's a phenomenon that is not just associated with the East Anglia region but all over the UK.

I have already covered the Hell-hound legend at Bungay in 1577, so will go onto other sightings of the alleged Black Shuck.

It appears that there are some tales that black dogs were associated to the witch trials, however some stories also depict the dogs in a good light too, such as an urban legend from a place called Littleport in

Cambridgeshire, where a young girl was being assaulted by a friar, and a black dog appeared as if from nowhere and scared off the friar thus saving the young girl from abuse. According to the legend the dog died in the attack and its spirit is left to wander the countryside as a protector.

Tales of the legendary black dogs (Shuck) were mostly spread through word and mouth, with one of the first legends being from the 11th & 12th Century Peterborough version of the Anglo Saxon Chronicles. It is alleged by one writer that a reliable witness had sworn to have seen packs of dogs that were jet black and had eyes like saucers and horrible, led in a wild hunt, by men on horseback, travelling through the woods from Peterborough heading towards Stamford. Could this be a medieval hunt or something more supernatural ?

However looking more closely into this tale it appears to be a tradition that spreads all over the UK and Europe and is known as the wild hunt. This is also a tale that may of sparked off the legends of The Black Shuck. No one will ever truly know for sure.

Northern cultures would associate the wild hunt with the change of seasons from Autumn to Winter and the strong winds that blow across the lands would howl as if from Hell hounds so it's no wonder legends of the Black Shuck was rife, as the sound was a sure way of insuring people to stay inside from the freezing weather coming in.

Sighting of the Black Shuck have reported right back from the 11th century to current dates, In 1905 a man in the west country claimed he witnessed a black dog turns into a donkey and then vanish a few heart beats later, another account of the black Shuck from a 4 year old girl during WWII claims she encountered a black Shuck, The large black dog walked from her window and around her bed, It made eye contact with its big red eyes and then disappeared before reaching the door.I am not really all that convinced by the sightings of the black Shuck, there are so many stories and theories out there, the most logical I have heard is that smugglers used to use dogs and the stories they would make up to scare people away from coastal regions to cover up their bootlegging operations. I do favour this explanation above others. Even if the smugglers let the dogs run wild and a few may run away more inland to account for those sightings. Its isn't hard to imagine.

Although as i draw a close on this short Blog, I'd like to share 1 last story with you.

I'm May 2014 at Leiston Abbey in Suffolk a skeleton was discovered or a giant dog, upon examination they likened the breed to be a Great Dane, It was suggested that it could be the remains of The Black Shuck that terrorised the area. The article I found stated that Carbon Dating was inconclusive, but I'm not sure if it has been tested again, and although the bones of the dog showed it was injured on the back leg, the archaeologists believe the dog was well kept. So it is unlikely to be a wild dog. So could this be the remains of the Black Shuck or a family pet. You decide.

If you would like to know more about The Black Shuck we at Parasearch have done a few shows on the subject so please click on or copy these links to have a listen.

https://www.spreaker.com/user/parasearchuk/special
-interview-mark-norman
And
https://www.youtube.com/watch?v=4m5DegmbDnc

Gargoyles : The Beginning.
Written by Paul Rook.

Have you ever taken a wander around a Gothic style building and glanced up towards the roof and witnessed a stone Gargoyle sitting there staring right back at you ? Have you wondered how they came about ?

There are many wonderful legends going back to the Roman and Greek era's regarding these horrifically ugly stone features, but the truth of the matter is that they are merely just Gothic works of art from the 13th century used to drain away water from the roof of a magnificent Gothic buildings and move it away from the walls as not to cause any structural damage. That is the truth behind them, The word 'Gargoyle' is derived from a French word 'Gargouille' which translated means 'Throat'.

Examples of Gargoyles have been discovered on the roof or both Egyptian and Greek temples and much like the Gothic medieval period very much served as a water spout, although with the Greek Temples sometimes the gargoyles were carved into other animals such as Lions.

Another theory as to why gargoyles were given their name comes from a legend in France of St Romanus or Romain, In this myth Romain was alleged to have rescued his country from a vile creature called Goji (Alleged to be Dragon Like), also known in some folk-tales as Gargouille. It was alleged that the creature was so grotesque that it would even repel off evil spirits. It was this legend that was thought to be the reason that the gargoyle stone features with various grimace faces became known in some parts as a protector thus explaining why they were placed on churches and other important buildings, one of which can still be seen today on The Tower of London.

Gargoyles were also used by the Catholic Church, many of the Pagan converts were illiterate so the church used the gargoyle as a sort of sermon in stone as a way of scaring the converts that they need to remain protected by the catholic church. It was just a lazy way of preaching instead of teaching the converts to read and write. Just a friendly reminder by the Church that if you don't go to church you will go to hell and suffer.

In the Celtic religion there is a legend that states that the Celts were headhunters and it was thought that the heads or their prey contained magical properties which defended them from evil. After killing their prey they would often put the heads on spikes and place them around their homes like trophies and this was said to repel evil and protect those within, and as the world evolved this practice turned into the more recognised images of the gargoyles faces on buildings.

I do believe the Gargoyle no matter what legend you know, were there to instil fear in people to turn to the church for protection in an illiterate period of history. Upon researching different types of Gargoyles around I found an article I would like to share its a list of the Top 10 facts about Gargoyles, here is just the last 2 taken from https://mentalfloss.com

During the restoration of Chapel of Bethlehem back in the early '90s, sculptor Jean-Louis Boistel decided to replace the building's crumbling gargoyles with a few pop-culture icons. This included Gizmo and a gremlin from the movie Gremlins, an Alien xenomorph, and a robot from the popular anime UFO Robot Grendizer. Many locals were put off by Boistel's creations, which are technically grotesques, but enough young movie fans got behind the "geek chapel" idea to get it approved.

Back in the '80s, the Washington National Cathedral held a contest for kids to design its newest gargoyle. Coming on the heels of the Star Wars trilogy, of course someone proposed a Darth Vader gargoyle. The cathedral, which had already installed some off-the-wall gargoyles and grotesques during its extensive restoration work, named 13-year-old Christopher Rader's design as one of its winners, and in 1986 put Lord Vader high up on the cathedral's "dark side" north wall. It can be difficult to spot, but the cathedral offers this handy guide.

Gargoyles are still popular today but not all these days are hideous monsters or vile water spewing heads, as already stated above we have Darth Vader, Alien and Gremlins, so next time your walking past a Gothic style building take a glance and see what you have staring back at you from the roof....Is it a gargoyle or something more humorous or even something from the movies !

The Missing 411
Written by Paul Rook.

On the 30th July, Kerry Greenaway and I hosted a show on the topic of the Missing 411. We were also joined by Psychologist Andy Mercer. I will post the link to the show at the end of this Blog. I also want to thank Mark Manley (The Alien Guy) from The Dark Mirror show (Friday Nights 9pm - 10pm on Parasearch Radio) for bringing this subject to the table, I found it amazingly fascinating.

Now for those of you that have never heard of The Missing 411, It is about people going missing in the National Forests of the U.S, however a Documentarian and Author by the name of David Paulides, Has has written a few books entitled The Missing 411 and made a few documentaries of the same name. David looked at over 12,000 cases if missing people in the national parks all over the US and he noticed that there are some familiar patterns in the disappearances of some of the cases for example some of the incidents happened in clusters within a small distance from each other. Some also had body's found in some interesting and mysterious circumstances, and some of the body's have never been found .... yet. The people that went missing ranged from 2 year old children to elderly adult hunters. so its not targeted to just 1 type of person.

Let's take a look at just 2 of the cases involved.

Stacey Arras was a typical 14 year old young lady, that enjoyed Horse Riding, One nice day in 1981 along with her father and one other they decided to take a camping trip on Horseback to Yosemite National Park, the party decided to stop over at Sunrise High Sierra Camp. The party of 3 pitched their camp and cleaned up. Stacey was also a keen photographer, and seeing as they were near to the lake there she asked her father and the 3rd person if they wanted to join her to take a look around the lake, they both declined, The lake wasn't that far from where they pitched their camp, in fact it was in ear shot, so off she went alone.

That was the last time she was ever seen, Stacey has never been found. After 9 days and an extensive search of the area nothing was found except the camera lens cap and nothing more. The search was comprised of over 100 ground searchers, helicopters ad sniffer dogs and nothing but the lens cap was discovered.

Another interesting case is one of Steven Kubacki.

At the time of this case Steven was 24 and it happened in February 1977. While he was Cross Country Skiing Steven decided that stopping near the edge of Lake Michigan. He remembers taking off his Skis so that he could take a break and sit and rest. But when he went to carry on with his journey the snow had covered his tracks so he became lost, The last thing he claims he remembered was walking through the snow feeling numb and exhausted, he was so exhausted he blacked out.

When he came round it was spring. He was laying in a typical grassy field in a forest clearing, Steven also remembers wearing clothed he didn't recognise as his own, he was also next to a strange looking back back which contained running shoes and glasses that was not his either.

Steven then got up and hiked to the nearest town, there he met a local resident and he enquired to where he was.
The local resident told him that he was in Pittsfield Massachusetts, 700 miles away from where he remembers skiing. Luckily Steven had family in Pittsfield, so he decided to visit his Aunt. As he knocked on the door his Aunt answered and was shocked that he was there and gave him a massive hug and asked where he had been all this time. Steven had been missing for 14 months.

Now going back 14 months to the time of the disappearance, Search teams were called in and during the search for Steven they found his skis at the edge of the lake and a set of footprints walking towards the lake, they did not find any footprints walking away from the site. Searchers could only assume that this was where Steven committed suicide and just walked into the freezing water. because Steven Kubacki was missing for so long he was presumed to be dead. Until he returned.

The official explanation for this case was Amnesia, But even Doctors are intrigued by this case as it's not all that common for someone to lose their memory for such a large junk of time. this case has even been studied by Psychologists, and even that community can not agree on what actually happened to Steven.

There are so many cases clubbed together to form the subject of Missing 411 so take a look at some of the others or watch documentaries or even read the books, and form your own conclusions, Alien Abductions, Ghostly Incidents, Time Slips,

Interdimensional Explanations, Faerie's or even Kidnappers and Murderers could all be explanations as to what is going on. what do you make of this subject ? I found it amazing and always never fails to fascinate me.

To listen to our podcast on this subject with Psychologist Andy Mercer please click or paste the link below to your URL .

https://www.spreaker.com/user/parasearchuk/paranormal-concept-missing-411

The Knights of St John
Written by Paul Rook.

As many people know, I am a proud member of the fine organisation St John Ambulance, I have served over 25 years now, and still have the passion to volunteer to work for them. I have given thousands of hours to my local community in their service, and as its something close to my heart, I thought I would share with you the history I am so proud to be a part of.

The Order of the Hospital of St John was founded around 1070, the sole responsibility was to care for the pilgrims during their pilgrimage to the Holy Lands. The Hospital was dedicated to St John the Baptist as he was seen as a healer of the mind and soul.

Although it was a hospital of sorts it was tended by monks and nuns and was finally recognised as a religious order in 1113, By Pope Paschal II and the order would tend the sick and injured no matter what faith the patients held.

The Brothers of the Hospital adopted the role of defending the Christians and when Jerusalem was lost in 1187 the Order of St John decided to establish their Headquarters in Acre just on the coast of Palestine. Due to wars and changing borders that occurred over the years they had to move Headquarters quite a few times, They moved from Acre to Cyprus then in 1309 went to Rhodes and in 1530 The Order of St John were gifted Malta to finally settle down as their new Headquarters. Then in 1798 The Order of St John were once again forced out of their Headquarters by Napoleon, then they were scattered to various other countries across Europe.

The order of St John were also a rival religious order to the Knights Templar, and when they were disbanded all their Treasures were given to The Order of St John

,... Well the stuff that wasn't hidden by the Knights Templar...but that's diverting from The Order of St John.

The Order had lots of land and property throughout western Europe, they were controlled by the local community of its members. They were called the Commanderies. It was their role to oversee the care of anyone that needed to be cared for. The communities were gathered into Provinces and this was known to the Order as Grand Priories. In Britain the communities was administered from a Commandery at Clerkenwell, London, from about 1140. They then became a Priory in 1185. It was also given the responsibility to run other Commanderies in Scotland, Wales and throughout England. Although Ireland was given the permission to become a separate Priory.

In 1540 the Order was combined with other monastic and religious organisations by King Henry VIII. However in 1557 Queen Mary I restored The Order of St John to be separated from other organisations. Then along came Queen Elizabeth I, and she ordered that all the Order of St John's estates be confiscated in 1559, and in 1564 the influence that the Reformation had had, ended the Orders activities in Scotland.

Now going back to the Roman Catholic Order of the Hospital of St John, which is now known as the Sovereign Military Hospitaller Order of St John of Jerusalem, Rhodes and of Malta (Also known as The Order of Malta) They survived the banishment from Malta and in 1820, their Knights, whom resided in France offered Knighthoods to its supporters in Great Britain no matter what their Christian Faith. This was something that the Order of Malta did not approve of. Much to the surprise of the Order of Malta the English Knights fully devoted themselves to the honourable cause and charitable activities.

With the Charitable Donations and wealth they accumulated The British Knights of the Order founded an Eye Hospital in Jerusalem in 1882, and in 1887 The Order had established St John Ambulance to train people in First Aid Skills. and in 1887 the volunteers were turned into a uniformed organisation so that their volunteers could serve at public events, they were known as the St John Ambulance Brigade. In 1888 all their hard work was rewarded when Queen Victoria recognised the Order and it became an Order of the British Crown.

In 1974 The Ambulance Association and the Brigade were combined together and became the St John Ambulance you know of today. In many parts of Britain, St John was the first and only provider of the Ambulance service right up until 1947 when the NHS was formed and they took over supplying the communities with their ambulance needs. Although St John Ambulance is still a Crown Service and backs up the NHS on a very regular basis. St John still attends many many public events and major sporting events, and even covers all royal family events. The Order of St John not only in the UK it operates in 30 countries around the world.

So now you know why I am very proud to serve in St John Ambulance, if it wasn't for them we may not have had the Ambulance Service we all rely on so much.

If you would like to learn more about the History of St John and go into more depth than I have for this blog then your welcome to visit The Museum of the Order of St John in St John's Gate London. It is free to get in and well worth taking a look. For more details on the museum please visit http://museumstjohn.org.uk

If you have a desire to join this wonderful organisation and live in the UK (Not Scotland) then please visit www.sja.org.uk For Scotland (St Andrews Ambulance) www.firstaid.org.uk

The information for this Blog was found on various St John Ambulance websites. So I would also like to Thank St John Ambulance.

H.G Wells & The War of the Worlds
Written by Paul Rook

This week we see the launch of the much anticipated adaptation of H.G Wells War of the Worlds.

H.G Wells happens to be one of my favorite authors.

For many years now we have enjoyed such novels as The Time Machine, The Invisible man & of course The War of the Worlds, just to name a few. I am sure that you have heard of most of his novels.

So let's go back to find out more about the man behind the war of the worlds...

Herbert George Wells was born was born in Bromley, in Kent on Friday 21st September 1866. He died

Tuesday August 13th 1946 in London. His father was Joseph Wells and his mother was called Sarah Neal. H,G Wells was known for various occupations including journalist, socialist and Historian but better known for his sci fi novels and short stories.

H.G Wells had a very hard youth as his parents were domestic servants, that worked for the owners of various small shops. His parents did everything they could to avoid becoming victims of poverty.

H.G Wells loved to read in his youth, and this helped him grow his knowledge base, as his education was very inadequate. At the age of 14 H.G Wells gained an apprenticeship to a Draper in Windsor, however soon after he was dismissed from service, H.G Wells then was offered various apprenticeships, one of which was to a chemist and another draper. In 1883 he became an usher at Midhurst Grammar School and at the age of 18 he was given a scholarship to study Biology and Darwinism under Thomas Henry Huxley at the normal school of science which later became the Royal College of Science . H.G Wells graduated from London University in 1888 and he became a science teacher and in 1891 H.G Wells married Isabel Mary Wells, who happened to be his cousin, but due to ill health and financial issues it exacerbated the marriage until H.G Wells met Amy Catherine Robbins who was one of his former pupils and then in 1895 Amy became his second wife,together they had 2 children called George Philip & Frank.

'Textbook of Biology' was H.G Wells first published book which was published in 1893. By 1895 H.G Wells launched his next book called The Time Machine and it the literary world by storm, this was his first science fiction book and this novel was just the first of a long line of science fiction that earned him the nickname of the Father of Science Fiction. The Time Machine was a book that propelled H.G Wells into public popularity. The book is about a scientist that creates a time travel machine, and is inspired by Science and Social aspects of the time, it also reaches the realms of the future class conflicts of evolution.

This novel has been adapted for 3 movies, 2 TV Shows and various comic books, it has also been the inspiration for lots of other works of fiction.

After a run of science fiction novels, in 1916 H.G Wells decided to try his hand at writing a few comedy novels, one of which was called Mr Britling Sees It Through and this was deemed by journalists as a masterpiece. described as a wartime experience in England.

H.G Wells was also well known for making scary predictions that came true. For example in another popular novel The World Set Free the characters split the atom thus creating the first Atomic Bomb.

H.G Wells loved to write, which he continued to do until the end of his life, but it was obvious that his attitude changed in his later novels towards his last days. He had a very dark outlook on life, his novel Mind at the end of its tether in 1945, was heavily criticized as it was about the end of humanity. However it was suggested that the reason he was so dark in this novel was down to his lack of good health and became very negative.

Now going back to the War of the Worlds, in 1897 the novel was split into a series of short weekly stories by Pearson's Magazine in the UK and Cosmopolitan in the United States.

War of the Worlds is a novel about the human race and the battle with an alien race for the right to populate the planet. The novel was well received and very popular however it did have its critics, some of which stated that it was very brutal in the nature of events that were narrated in style.

According to the spokesman of the H. G. Wells Society, writer Emelyne Godfrey, "The War of the Worlds is a critique of imperialism and man's hubris." The writer explained to OpenMind that Wells was influenced by The Battle of Dorking, a fictional German invasion of Britain published in 1871 by George Tomkyns Chesney.

And now the BBC has adapted the War of the Worlds and is currently on Sundays at 9pm. If you want to know more about this novel please listen to our podcast by using the below URL.

Dementia & The Paranormal
Written by Paul Rook

As always I never miss an episode of Casualty, I
noticed that in the episode aired on Saturday 30th
November, one of the main characters that is
currently undergoing a dementia storyline and
playing the part of the sufferer in the beginning
stages, began to hallucinate a cat that she had
when she was younger, it then made me think,
would it be feasible for dementia patients to see
spirit ?

According to the NHS website it is possible 'a
person with Dementia may lose empathy
(understanding and Compassion), they may see

or hear things that other people do not (Hallucinations).' - www.nhs.uk

According to the Alzheimer's Society there are around 850,000 people in the UK with dementia. One in 14 people over 65 will develop dementia, and the condition affects 1 in 6 people over 80.

The number of people with dementia is increasing because people are living longer. It is estimated that by 2025, the number of people with dementia in the UK will have increased to around 1 million.

Those facts and figures were also taken from the NHS website, It's scary to think that something so awful is so common.

What Causes Dementia ?

Dementia isn't a single disease. Dementia is a term used to describe the symptoms that occur when there's a decline in brain function. Several different diseases can cause dementia. Many of these diseases are associated with an abnormal build-up of proteins in the brain.This build-up causes nerve cells to function less well and ultimately die. As the nerve cells die, different areas of the brain shrink.

Causes of Alzheimer's disease.

Alzheimer's disease is the most common type of dementia. In the brain of someone with Alzheimer's disease, there are two different proteins called amyloid and tau. Deposits of amyloid, called plaques, build up around brain cells. Deposits of tau form "tangles" within brain cells.
Researchers don't yet fully understand how amyloid and tau are involved in the loss of brain cells, but this is an area of active research.

As brain cells become affected in Alzheimer's, there's also a decrease in chemical messengers (called neurotransmitters) involved in sending messages, or signals, between brain cells. Levels of one neurotransmitter, acetylcholine, are particularly low in the brains of people with Alzheimer's disease. Medicines like donepezil increase levels of acetylcholine, and improve brain function and symptoms. These treatments aren't a cure for Alzheimer's disease, but they do help improve symptoms.

The symptoms that people develop depend on the areas of the brain that have been damaged by the disease. The hippocampus is often affected early on in Alzheimer's disease. This area of the brain is responsible for laying down new memories. That's why memory problems are one of the earliest symptoms in Alzheimer's.
Unusual forms of Alzheimer's disease can start with problems with vision or with language.

Causes of vascular dementia

Vascular dementia is caused by reduced blood flow to the brain. Nerve cells in the brain need oxygen and nutrients from blood to survive. When the blood supply to the brain is reduced, the nerve cells function less well and eventually die.

Reduced blood flow can be caused by:

narrowing of the small blood vessels deep inside the brain – known as small vessel disease (subcortical vascular dementia); this is the main cause of vascular dementia and is more common in people who smoke, or have high blood pressure or diabetes a stroke (where the blood supply to part of the brain is suddenly cut off, usually as a result of a blood clot) – called post-stroke dementia lots of "mini strokes" that cause widespread damage to the brain – known as multi-infarct dementia
Not everyone who's had a stroke will go on to develop vascular dementia.

Causes of frontotemporal dementia

This is an important cause of dementia in younger people. It's most often diagnosed between the ages of 45 and 65.

It's caused by an abnormal clumping of proteins, including tau, in the frontal and temporal lobes at the front and sides of the brain. The clumping of these proteins damages nerve cells in the frontal and temporal lobes, causing brain cells to die. This leads to shrinking of these areas of the brain. Frontotemporal dementia is more likely to run in families and have a genetic link than other, more common causes of dementia. - https://www.nhs.uk/conditions/dementia/causes/

With that all in mind, Isn't it plausible that some of the hallucinations could be visiting spirits ? When parts of the brain are affected some Dementia sufferers can relive parts of their childhood.

We also see a connection to young children being able to see and hear spirits, I personally believe that their young brains are more susceptible to spirit because it's still underdeveloped, so with a brain of a Dementia patient could it be that their brains are almost deconstructed to the point where they become under developed enough to pick up on spirits, and that would explain why dementia patients talk to and hallucinate people from their lives that have passed.

However looking more into what happens to the brain when we hallucinate i discovered that although medical science understand why, and what happens to some people that hallucinate, medical science does not know how these events happen in the brain. This is something a team of researchers at the University of Oregon was a mystery that they tried to answer, and discover how the brain was affected.

The researchers used mice for their experiments into hallucinations and their findings were somewhat surprising.
They injected a special drug into the mice, which made them hallucinate. This drug is commonly

used in the world of animal testing. The drug affected the mouse visual cortex, which is the part of the brain that takes and sorts images we see and converts them into information for the brain. So these mice were stoned off their nuts...

The results of the tests were interesting, the researchers expected to see an increase of neurons in the mouse visual cortex to be firing at fast speeds, however this was not the case. But it was also noted that the control mice also received the same activity in the visual cortex without the drugs, thus concluding that the mice were receiving the information but the visual cortex could not process it correctly.

Now if we applied that information to someone with dementia, could they still hallucinate a spirit ? If the visual cortex is affected by dementia then could it just be that the person suffering is just recalling a memory and seeing it play out. So it would appear to someone in the same room as them that they are seeing a spirit from the past, but is in actual fact a confused signal to the visual cortex.

It is a concept that I will be looking into further and be putting together a show on Parasearch Radio and discussing this possibility with a Doctor and Psychologist in the near future. It would be interesting to get your opinions on my thoughts.

Kerry Greenaway
Co Owner

Kerry Greenaway is the owner of Spirit & Soul Island Crystals which specializes in selling Crystal and Mineral specimens. She has been involved in energy and spiritual work for the past 30yrs starting off by reading Tarot Cards which then evolved into working intuitively with Crystals.

Kerry has always had an interest in the supernatural and paranormal and loved nothing better than to curl up with a good book about the subject. When paranormal TV first hit the media it opened a new area of interest of actually being able to go out into the field and investigate. About 5yrs ago she was invited onto a paranormal investigation and utilised her spiritual skills within the field.

This led to being interviewed on a radio show and led her down a new pathway of Parasearch Radio. Kerry is now co-owner and Presenter the station exploring many topics on the supernatural and paranormal. This has led her to interviewing leading figures in the paranormal field as well as in the spiritual bringing a wide range of experiences and knowledge to her listeners. Kerry now classes herself as more of a researcher than an investigator as the thirst for knowledge is her first passion. However she is still known to venture out occasionally. Not only that but Kerry regularly writes blogs for the Parasearch Radio

Tarot Cards
Written by Kerry Greenaway.

Tarot Readings are a form of divination using a specialised deck of cards that outlines potential outcomes and looks at the influences surrounding a person, event or both. They are a personal form of guidance and it should always be remembered that the future is subject to change as you have free will and can only focus on the possible outcomes.

The origins of the Tarot deck are steeped in mystery but we do know it originated from cartomancy which is where playing cards were used as a form of divination but in regards to Tarot who designed them, where they came from or when they first started is unknown although many myths and legends surround them.

The earliest known tarot decks weren't designed with mystercism in mind they were designed as a card game similar to modern day Bridge. They first entered Europe in the late 14th century. The oldest surviving Tarot Deck was owned by the Visconti Sforza family who were rulers of Rome These forms of deck were only used by the privileged and rich as at this time they were hand painted. They were used in a game called Tarocchi Appropriati, where random cards were dealt and they used the symbology within the cards to make up stories.

The divinitary use of the Tarot really took off in the 1700's. In 1791 Jean Baptiste Alliette (Etteille) wrote a book on the art of reading the cards as a form of divination. Etteille was the first to issue a full tarot deck with 78 cards two main sections, the major (greater secrets) and minor (lesser secrets) arcana.

Etteille was a french Occultist who first brought the idea of the four elements and astrology into the deck. He is the first known person to have made a living out of reading tarot as a form of divination and thanks to his book – A way to entertain yourself with a deck of cards- made tarot more accessible and popular.

With the event of Industrial revolution and the invention of the printing press, tarot decks became more affordable and accessible and during this period became a popular parlour game. The real resurgence of Tarot occurred in the 19th century alongside the interest of the Occult, magic and the esoteric. In 1909 the Rider Waite Tarot became available and is still one of the most popular decks printed today.

There are literally hundreds of decks now available covering every form of genre, symbology, historical and pop culture and it can be hard to decide what deck to choose to work with. My opinion is that choose a deck that you feel intuitively drawn to, one that symbology you resonate with, go with your gut feeling. There is a train of thought that you shouldn't purchase your own deck, personally I don't agree with this point and don't see that it matters either way, if the person is buying it for you and they know you well then they will probably choose wisely and the chances are you will resonate with it.

When learning to read a tarot deck the best place to start is with the little book that comes with them. Learn the general meanings first, if you try to learn the whole 78 cards off by heart you will end up losing the intuitive side of yourself so start by giving yourself a general overview about what each suit means and the various stages the cards take you through. There are loads of myths surrounding how to attune your energies together from sleeping with the deck to kissing the deck once you've finished working with it. One thing I do know for sure is that you do need to treat the deck like a sentient being much in the same way we talk about crystals, be appreciative and show gratitude after each time you work with the deck and you will soon find you begin to understand the deeper meanings behind each card.

Next time I shall delve a little deeper into what the Major and Minor Arcana teaches us.

For an interesting and in depth discussion on Tarot have a listen to the show done with Ashley Mortimer and Steve Ward.

https://www.spreaker.com/user/parasearchuk/the-sp
irit-dimension-the-fools-journey

Conspiracy
Written by Kerry Greenaway

On Parasearch recently we've been looking in Conspiracy theories so that got me thinking about where they come from and how situations develop into this way of thinking.

A conspiracy is a secret plan by a group to do something unlawful or harmful, the conscious action of plotting or conspiring

There are three main psychological factors at play here

Epistemic – Understanding our environment – relating to knowledge or to the degree of validation

Existential – Being safe and in control of our environment – affirming or implying the existence of a thing

Social – Our place within our environment & maintaining a positive self image with this structure.

Conspiracy Theories are usually born out of events where there is no definitive clear cut explanation which pulls those three factors (Epistemic, Existential & Social) into question. Any situation where there are inconsistencies and contradictions triggers our insecurities and we are unable to achieve a state called cognitive closure. This means that humans desire to eliminate ambiguity and arrive at a definitive conclusion. Historical precedents of situations have created a level of distrust and people are no longer taking things on face value and are scrutinising situations in greater depth than ever before- but are they?

In a study of Joe Parent & Joe Usinski in 2014 they randomly selected 104,803 letters published in the New York Times and the Chicago Tribune between 1890 – 2010 for the conspiracy theory mindset. The results were interesting and showed no obvious trend rises. There were two notable spikes in the data. The first in 1900 around the time of the 2nd Industrial revolution and the second in the late 40's/early 50's which was around the beginning of the cold war.

Conspiracy theories are usually linked to political affiliation and belief systems and this often leads to ignoring scientific evidence in favour of these affiliations – basically people only believe what fits their theory. The other factor to consider is media influence, you only have to look at the drip feed media frenzy of a breaking story to witness wild misinformation, jumps of assumption and unvalidated witness statements. It's hardly surprising that conspiracy theories arise.

When I first started researching this topic, I assumed it was a modern creation born out of readily available information and armchair experts but I was soon proved wrong. One of the earliest conspiracy theories was actually way back in AD 64 and surrounded the Great Fire of Rome.

This particular situation started on the 18th July and lasted for about 1 week, it all but leveled Rome, Nero was the Emperor of the day and at the time was out of town at his country residence. He did return to Rome but the timing of this is questionable.

A conspiracy theory started to circulate that Nero had been compliant in starting the fire so that he could rebuild Rome to his own design and Nero hadn't cared when Rome was burning and had in fact been singing and playing his fiddle at the time. Nero retaliated with a counter conspiracy stating that the Christians (at this time they were a sub-cult in Rome) had started the fire in order to undermine Rome's Governance and Beliefs.

Nero didn't really help himself as following the fire he went onto build Demus Aurea, a majestic series of villas with landscaped parks and manmade lakes. He built this on part of the site of the fire. Also the timing of this is relevant as it buys into the theory that Nero actually started the fire to remodel Rome in his own vision. Having said this Nero did not escape unscathed from the fire – the Forum and his palace Domus Transitoria was also burnt to the ground. The stories surrounding his return to Rome are also a little misleading, he did return to Rome not only to help with the post fire aid but to also help with the firefighting efforts. What lends credence to the anti-Nero conspiracy is the general living conditions of the populace of Rome , the majority of people lived in slums,

wooden structures not the grand stone structures people imagine. It was a long desired objective of many people who felt subjected or oppressed to effectively bring Rome down. Christians hadn't really helped the situation as pre fire they had circulated vengeful texts predicting that a raging inferno would reduce the city to ashes – the theme of Rome must burn was prevalent at this time.

Following the fire Nero's accusations against the Christian caused widespread persecution and rumour has it ordered that Christians should be rounded up and killed – it is well known that many Christians were killed in the most horrific manner after this time.

Basically the facts of the matter are Rome burning was an accident waiting to happen and both sides tried to manipulate the situation to their own advantage unfortunately in this case Nero had the majority of power control.

Leaping ahead let's take a look at a more recent conspiracy theory – Climategate

In Nov 2009 an external hacker hacked into a server at the climatic research unit at the University of East Anglia, they went onto post these documents and e-mails to various locations across the internet. These were picked up but the climate change denialists, they argued that the emails showed that global warming was a scientific conspiracy and that scientists had manipulated climate data in order to suppress those who denied it was happening.

The timing of this was a key factor as in Dec 2009 the Climate Change Mitigation commenced – this is where 115 world leaders attended to discuss global warming and put into place structures and litigation to help combat it. It was stated that the release of these documents or timed hack of the documents was done to undermine the conference. After all if there was no climate change then there would be no need for the powers that be to do anything – backing up the climate change denialists perspective.

Basically the documents suggested that scientists had manipulated the data to support claims of a sudden increase in the earth's temperature. They had suppressed evidence that contradicted the anthropogenic global warming hypothesis I.e where humans are causing the changes in the environment.

They had disguised facts about the medieval period when the earth was warmer that it is today and also suppressed opposing scientific opinions in the peer review process.

As you can imagine this caused a huge political/scientific and media storm with many opposing views and cross propaganda which still has repercussions in today's society. The main consensus is still confused regarding global warming and the damage this caused was insurmountable.

One thing's for sure you only have to open your eyes to see how humans are destroying and polluting the plant and something needs to be done.

In the minds of the everyday person this has led to deeper distrust of the government, politics, economics and scientists so it's hardly surprising conspiracy theories abound particularly when they pull into question our understanding of our environment, feeling safe and our place in the world.

There are many precedents of cross propaganda surrounding today's society – most commonly known these days as 'Fake News' – you just have to have a look at The Corpse factories from WW1 – this was a fabricated story by head of intelligence John Charteris – to see political manipulation in action. If you would like to hear more about this then I refer you to :-

The Spirit Dimension – Remembrance Show. https://www.youtube.com/watch?v=bvoAN236nWU

In today' society with the widely available access to information fake news or conspiracy theories travel further and faster than ever before and you can find 'evidence' to support all kinds of situations leaving the general public in a quagmire of misinformation, misdirection and distrust of any so called experts in the field. Even if the truth was put out there totally unembellished it would be called into question.

So where does that leave us? Be discerning, do your own research, look at all sides of the augment and try to place your personal belief systems on hold whilst doing so. Most importantly maintain reason and logic and some basic common sense because at the end of the day ..... is it really important to your own personal life if man really did walk on the moon?

Demons
Written By Kerry Greenaway

Let's talk about demons – OMG #Demon is a regular on tv shows but let's take a look at the whole concept of demons, gasp !!

The origin of the word actually comes from Greece and comes from the word Eudaimonia which literally translates to good spiritness. They viewed these as spirits of the dead and deities and worshipped them on altars within their home as they did with many other idols of gods and goddesses. They were the epitome of the tutelary spirit that we looked at in my previous blog – Do we create paranormal activity part

2.

http://www.parasearch.org/b/are-we-creating-parano rmal-activity--part-2

When Christianity took hold, the general belief system changed from many god's to the supreme god and they viewed these many deities as heathen idols and this began the perception of negativity. Nowhere in the bible does it state that they are fallen angels however various scriptures outline the need to banish /exorcise these kinds of spirits and use the word Demon in connection to them. However, interpretations of the bible by its leaders gave the hierarchy of the Demons to being minions to Satan. Much like Angels being the deliverers of good things, demons were the deliverers of the bad stuff. Now that is a very brief synopsis of the origins of the word but it gives you a general idea of the evolution of a belief/word.

The rise of Christianity was a huge reason why the connotations regarding these types of entity changed into negativity however there are references to them across many cultures.

The Egyptians viewed these kind of spirits into two categories wanderers and guardians – the guardians were assigned a specific place (genius loci) and the wanderers were the ones to watch out for they served justice or retribution from the Gods and not in a good way, they bought death, disease and misfortune, not quite as cosy as the Greeks viewpoint.

In all faith based religions there is a tiered system – Head God, Council of Gods, Demigods, Minions of God, Elemental Spirit/Humans with variations of this theme. Also this then splits into two sides, the same ranking for both positive and negative. Note we are the lowest on the list and at the mercy to the whims and desires of the Gods. Whilst we are at it I'd just like to address Elementals quickly – these are spirits that are attached to a specific element and are godless, they are tied to nature and have neither a benevolent or malevolent energy, but more on this another time.

Demons being classed as minions of God, in fact go back far enough, there are references to these kinds of entities, they are not good and are embodied in the negative traits seen within humans. Such as greed, jealousy, envy etc – sound familiar. The melting pot of all of these religions being distilled into one religion I.e christianity makes it hardly surprising that demons took on a negative trait.

The rise and fall of various religious mythologies is the main reason why there is a misunderstanding of these lesser entities, one thing's for sure, I doubt very much if you will find one hanging in the nearest haunted location!

No matter how you view Demons one thing's for sure they are prevalent in belief system in every culture through the ages. Are they there very own independent spirit or are they from within and used for blame when we as people show negative traits. We all fight these inner negative demons so

is it a case of externalising these traits into an entity?

One thing is clear various origins do not depict these 'entities' as bad or evil in any way its a religious based perception that has coloured the word. Nowadays the internet is full of demonologists and lists of names of various alleged demons or attachments by these kind of entities so it's hardly surprising that deep within we have a fear or even down right skepticism regarding this topic.

Witch Finders
Written by Kerry Greenaway

If I said the term Witchfinder General to you then the first name to pop up in your head would be Matthew Hopkins notorious in history for his part in the witch trials.

Firstly before we begin this sordid tale then we have to bare in mind the religious and political background.

In Scotland, things were not so good for witches under the reign of James VI, he took a keen interest in witch trials and considered himself to be an expert in the field. He wrote Daemonologie in 1597 and left a trail of witch hunts and persecution behind him when he came to England. He was the first of the Stuarts reign in England succeeding as James 1st of England after Elizabeth 1st died without an heir.

Now it's worth bearing in mind at this point that the Christian belief was that a Witch made a pact with the Devil deliberately and did not act alone. So basically if you find one then there was always more. As you can imagine this took the focus away from the 'strange healer' of the village to a heady association is guilt approach. Not only that but there was no difference between black or white magic both were viewed as bad as each other.

The political landscape at that time was turbulent to say the least, England was going through a civil war with two extremely opposing views. the Parliamentarians versus the Monarchy. The whole country was in a state of social unrest with poverty, famine and plague. Religion had also been thrown into uncertainty, with factions split into sides — protestant/roman catholic = Monarchy, Puritans = Parliamentarians. Not only this but in the outlying villages and towns the strength of these alliances weakened and you were met with varying levels of belief systems including older more pagan beliefs. These are the undercurrents and effects on day to day life that everybody faced so it's not hard to understand that old jealousy, slights and feuds raised there head.

In regards to witch hunting, this was nothing new, especially in Europe, if you look into the case of witch finders such as Julius Echter von Mespelbrunn or Nicholas Eymerich along with various publications such as 1376 Directorium Inquisitoria, incidentally written by Nicholas, then its hardly surprising that at some point it would infect the UK. In 1612 Sebastian Michaels a French inquisitor wrote The admirable history of possession and conversion of a penitent woman. A few years before our very own James 1st was also overly concerned with witches writing Daemonologie in 1597 and leaving a trail of witch trials behind him in Scotland when he came to England so it's hardly surprising that the surge in witch hunting took a leap at this time. In 1613 James passed a law stating the death penalty for anyone proved to have caused harm through witchcraft or magic.

Generally the hunting of witches was a distasteful business to the lords and priests of the area, they had loftier concerns at hand, raised taxes, general unrest and the poverty of the times dictated this and quite frankly didn't have the time or concern to go about the business of proof of witches, it was a matter of folklore and superstition. All of a sudden a new job opportunity opened up and it suddenly became a lucrative way of earning a living!

An original complaint against a person for witchcraft would always come from the local populace, the local leader would then call in a witchfinder to find the proof that this was the case. Its in this environment that John Stearne and Matthew Hopkins take the lead roll. The witch finders job was to find proof under the remit of the law, bearing in mind torture had been abolished in 1640. Firstly the accused was body searched looking for feeding teats or witches mark, this wasn't done by the witch finders themselves but would be done by men and women employed for the task such as local midwife's or well standing men. If such a mark was found then the witch finder would step in and the process of getting a confession would start, a series of deprivations and scrutiny would start. First the accused would be seated on a stool and watched, they would be denied food, water, sleep or comfort breaks. It doesn't sound too tortuous does it but imagine the situation, a person already under nourished and dehydrated, probably been rough handled, in fear for your life just being watched for a devil imp to appear for feeding. These 'imps' would appear in many forms, a beetle, a mouse, a fly anything living coming near you was considered evidence that you were a witch. This treatment would continue with bouts of verbal abuse, compelling you to confess your sins, everything was done to effectively push a person to the limits of their physical and mental well being. If the first step did not achieve the required result then the accused was walked until they collapsed then walked some more. A key point you have to remember is that they were not looking to prove the accused had performed any magick but that they had made a pact with the devil. A confession to this was what they were after and got. Not only that but the belief was that when you found one witch you found others so the drive to name others or accomplices was apparent in the questioning. As soon as that confession was obtained then the accused was put into a local gaol, moved into a main prison ready for the Assizes basically the court and trial, the Witch finder would then present the evidence and off he would go onto another village or town employed to hunt for the next witch. Whole villages were decimated by suspicion, accusation and jealousies.

A couple of points here – water dunking was frowned upon but still used on the odd occasion, there are a couple of references in regards to Hopkins but it wasn't his usual method. It was eventually banned in 1645. Bleeding – basically cutting a person with a blunt knife – if they did not bleed then they were a witch – there are no verified records of Hopkins using this method. Hopkins prefered to break the spirit of an already weakened person, he was a person's worst fear – a bully with power! In regards to the death penalty in England, hanging was the method, the images of witches burning at the stake are all from the Europe inquisitions. There are a couple of cases where women were burned at the stake however it was not because of witchcraft but because they murdered their husband!

Hopkins and Stearne became infamous in history due to their exploits within the witch trails in Essex, the number of men and women accused in Essex alone reached over 200 people and excessive amount compared to other counties.

Also this is incredible when you consider the alleged age of Hopkins 25yrs, this is an estimate as we have no birth records. His reign of terror only lasted for approx 13-18 months there are varying accounts depending on the source, after which he sank back into obscurity. So one wonders why this happened, well the witch finder wasn't beyond criticism or accusation themselves. Their methods of obtaining confession drew the attention of high ranking officials and were even accused of being witches themselves, after all how comes they are so good at finding witches unless they themselves have made a pact!

Matthew Hopkins is actually a very enigmatic figure in himself, in fact any information about him is conjecture or assumption until 1641, he has no birth certificate, academic records and there are only vague references for this period. The belief is that he worked in Law and lived in Mistley after

growing up in Manningtree. His age is a guesstimate and there is only one reference in death records stating he died on 12th August 1647 and is buried in Mistley. He has become a shadowy figure in history, forever lost in the mists of time, surrounded by myths and legends.

Whenever we look back at history you have to bare fully in mind the time period and external influences being played out on whichever personage or situation you are researching. The witch trials were built on political and social unrest, power and religion. Emotional responses were based on fear and survival.

To try and understand the witch trials you have to try to transport yourself back to that time period, imagine the day to day struggle for a meal where your physical well being is dependent on if you live or die, god forbid you fall ill! Social standing is based on wealth, who you married and your character is judged on how many times you go to church or your political opinion. These factors matter so we not only learn the facts and figures of a case but actually understand it.

This is one of the reasons the paranormal is so interesting to me it encompasses so many angles and avenues, rabbit holes if you will. I first started looking at Matthew Hopkins when I was looking into writing the Demon Blog, the devil imps being proof that someone was a witch interested me so I was following that line of enquiry. Of course I knew about Matthew Hopkins, I do live in Essex after all, I had heard the stories, but I haven't researched him in depth. What I found out was surprised me and horrified me. Witch hunt mentality happens to this day, we see it played out on social media and the broader media spectrums.

The only difference is that society has evolved or has it!!

Love in the Paranormal Field
Written by Kerry Greenaway.

I was thinking about 'Love' that elusive enigmatic emotion that can be felt and expressed in so many ways and yet we are unable to measure it. It may be an act or an involuntary gesture that makes you feel, really feel, this emotion . It is as distant and remote as the moon yet has such an effect on our daily lives in so many ways. It is built from experiences and knowledge of self, your personal insecurities, needs , wants, that creates the emotion of 'Love'. Can we measure it? I stated before that it is immeasurable and this is true we can't measure the depth or breadth of how the emotion feels. What we can do is measure the physical responses when we feel this emotion, effectively we are measuring the effect of the emotion not the trigger or the cause. It is different for every single one of us and yet we all feel it at some point in our lives.

Researching the paranormal is a journey down many of those infamous rabbit holes that can lead in multiple directions and lead you into an avenue you never expected to go. It is a field filled with theories that are unproven by science and opinions. It can be enlightening and enthralling and frustrating and confusing in equal measure. It is a field when the normal working man crosses paths with scientists and academia, a field where mass media crosses paths with morals and ethics , a field where personal opinion and experience crosses swords with belief systems and culture. All of this you take on, a quest if you will. A quest to prove life exists after death, that we have an eternal consciousness, that we have meaning !

I have had the enormous pleasure of speaking to many people in the field from all sides of the paranormal spectrum and I can honestly say that it has been the source of my own personal spiritual and paranormal journey. From these discussions and I can say with confidence that there is no one size fits all, that everybody has something to offer as crazy or diverse as that may be. That everybody has their own pathway in this amazingly weird world we decide to spend our time within. What brings people into the field usually boils down to two replies, the first is a personal experience that remains unexplained within the recesses of your mind, an experience that usually happened within the informative childhood years. The other is having watched main stream media paranormal tv show or documentary, a film or book that reignited the spark within of a quest.

With the birth of the internet the paranormal world is more accessible than ever. We can watch investigation after investigation. We can live debate what is being seen and give our opinions on what we are witnessing. We can listen to multiple podcasts (Parasearch is the obvious go to for listening pleasure) covering topics more wide and diverse than any other field. We can read blogs, magazines and books galore on the subject. We can join long standing institutes that have researched and studied varying phenomena from hundreds of years. A bombardment if you will from every angle on the subject .

So where does that leave us, usually confused and bewildered.

So we come back to the concept of 'Love' , that elusive to explain emotion. I see it within the field, people Love what they do, there is passion and excitement , a thirst for knowledge, genuine emotion for other people you work with, the thrill of a new book in your hand. It is unmeasurable and just like a personal experience impossible to explain. This is why we stepped into the field in the first place and its important to remember your own personal reason why you do what you do. There are no hard and fast rules, this is your journey of experience and learning and you walk that path at your own speed and in the way you wish to proceed. After all you only have to answer to your own conscience.

Ah I bought 'conscience' into the room! – that moral yardstick of right and wrong.

This paranormal field will always court controversy and heated debate but within that we must always remember the impact of words , the human behind the keyboard or within the situation. Bring knowledge, respect and integrity to the field. Act accordingly with your own conscience and surround yourself with like minded people. That is the way forward in the field, it is a personal journey and one that can be taken in many directions with love and passion.

A Perfect Storm
Written By Kerry Greenaway

A perfect storm is a rare combination of events or circumstances creating an unusually
bad situation.
This is exactly what I thought when I listened to Lori Shafer talking about an experience she
had when she and team mates investigated .... although in this case the perfect storm
didn't result in a bad situation but an encounter with a spirit who connected to the people

involved. The belief being that the cultural and language skills in the group were the perfect

combination to allow the spirit to connect. The question is was it really just a question of the

language and culture or was something more going on?

Previously we have discussed the theory that the perfect energy, frequency and vibration is

required to make that connection to spirit or to cross dimensions. This is not a new theory

and has been bandied about for quite some time so let's examine this in further depth.

It brought to mind a workman, now workmen have a special affinity with the tools they

work with. They have a favourite screwdriver or paintbrush something I myself have

encountered when renovating two houses, in my case it was a chair. Now that chair was old

and battered however it was the perfect height and had the perfect sturdiness, I trusted it

would not collapse when I stood on it, it was the right weight, I could move it around with ease etc etc.

There was nothing special about that chair but I was possessive over it and

every time I redecorated, that chair would be an essential part of the decorating process, in

effect I had a connection to that battered old chair in that particular circumstance and after

the task was completed it would go back into the garage until the next time. When the time

came that the chair finally gave up the ghost it was a sad day. Since then nothing has

replaced that chair, a ladder simply doesn't cut the mustard and I have yet to find another

chair that fits the bill quite so well as that old decorating chair does. My connection to that

chair may seem a little bizarre when reading this but I'm sure many can relate whether in

this circumstance or another.

The ability of connection is unique to humans, we take ownership of inanimate objects and

make them our own, it inspires possessiveness, we form a relationship with them far beyond

anything that logic, reason and practicality would suggest. This ownership is especially seen
in the spiritual field. When choosing a spiritual tool we are searching for that instant
connection, for example when choosing pendulum we are looking for that strength of
connection and the belief being it is shown in the strength of the swing, or a tingle in the
hand, or the intangible it just feels right - a connection of energy perhaps?
Connection - a relationship in which a person or thing is linked or associated with something
else.

Humans form connections for many different reasons and this in turn leads to a relationship, my
connection to that old chair was emotional on some level, it was born from it's unique
physiology, practicality and exactly fitted the circumstances it was needed for. It didn't matter if
paint got on it or the cushion was slightly ripped it served its purpose exactly within the premise

of my own personal need in that circumstance and I was sad when the chair was beyond repair
and yes every time I decorate I still to this day miss that old chair.
People form many kinds of connection throughout their lives and for many different reasons.
When it is with another sentient being we call this a relationship. Now I could waffle on about
different forms of relationship but one formed under investigation in the paranormal world starts
with the very basic – shared interest.

This is where it starts, the coming together of a group of people with a common goal of going
out into various locations to try and contact spirit, to get the evidence and to prove that there is
life after life that we do go on and that we have a purpose. We are emotionally involved, it
challenges our belief systems and pushes us on to learn and evolve. Through this relationships
are formed and when the 'vibe' is right there is no beating it, everybody in the group feels

secure in knowing their own personal function, status and is confident within themselves and

this is what makes it special. That unique connection that leads us to terms such as 'parafamily'

or 'tribe'. This can happen over a long period of time or it can be quite immediate as in the case

of Lori's experience.

The assumption that they had that experience purely because of cultural and linguistic abilities

created the right frequency to allow the spirit to communicate may well be underestimated. Now

I'm not saying this isn't a factor as I certainly believe it is but I think it may go deeper than that.

The connection the people involved had to each other may well also be a factor and something

that we need to consider more on the field. That instance of connection and the strength of that

connection should not be underestimated, we've all felt it and have little chance of

understanding it. What is it exactly that creates that instant like or dislike for another person?

When people come together, all with their own personal energy signature that resonates with
another energy signature in perfect unison, different yet together creates a harmony and this
may well be the intangible frequency that helps to create the perfect storm.

Sensationalism
Written By Kerry Greenaway

I read an article completely unrelated to the paranormal however the title was sensationalised to the hilt and I thought to myself that everything is hyped up to the max, words taken out of context and situations are blown into something they are not. This is not a new phenomenon, when we researched for the remembrance show we came across tales of black propaganda all designed to spur the British forwards in the fight against atrocity. This brought to mind some of my own words criticizing the sensationalization of paranormal stories in order to sell locations.

And it does sell, whether a book, tv show, newspaper or a location!

What it also does is dilute facts, present a specific perception, in effect it tells you what to think. They do this by collecting data. Just about every form you fill in, the transaction you make, post on social media goes into this data collection and from this they then target advertise what they want you to see. Don't believe me then take a look at 'The Great Hack' on Netflix which details the Cambridge Analytical Scandal.

This leads into two minds, people who take what they are exposed to and don't question it, this leads to believing the information presented is true. The second mind of people is people who question it and look into it more to try to find out the real facts behind the case.

We see this time and time again in the paranormal field. So do we believe the hype of a haunting? Or do we dig deeper and try to find out the fundamental questions that need to be asked. How much true, real research is being done beyond what we have at our fingertips.

Are we taking everything at face value and listening to regurgitated stories of experiences people have had whilst out and then having the same experiences? Are we disappointed when nothing happens and then dismissive of the locations or story and just move onto the next? Are we just purely interested in capturing something on camera or for personal experience? Are we just out for the thrill of the hunt?

I see many themes running through the paranormal field and people working at many different levels throughout the field. You cannot compare a blogger with an academic, nor a small team with an event evening, or a private investigation to a location-based investigation. However, what we can do is talk to each other. The ghost investigation teams are regularly out in the field and with a little guidance from the academics may well be able to collect the data needed to help find the patterns that can try and provide some of the answers we are all searching for. Likewise if dealing with a private investigation, reach out to talk to people there is a wealth of information that can be utilised and this is exceptionally important in regards to 'helping'.

What we need to be aware of is the need to sensationalise everything to the point where the facts get lost, and even if they are there can't be seen amongst the deluge of false information. We need to be able to think about how information is presented and be open to any questions others may have.

We need to dig deeper, read more, communicate, ask questions, look beyond the screen in front of you and do the same in libraries, talk to local historians, records offices. Etc.

This field is an amazing way of expanding your personal knowledge in so many different areas and I urge you look beyond the sensationalized headline and look to the fundamentals of a case, it's usually more strange than the headline!

Alone in the dark ?
Written By Kerry Greenaway

You're sitting alone in a dark cold cellar with only a piece of paranormal gadget in your hand waiting for that elusive personal experience. This is the norm for most paranormal teams out there but do we have to investigate in the dark? This is a concept that is talked about time and time again in the field.

From the early days of spiritualism séances were only ever conducted in the Dark with either a candle – preferably a red one and then later on a red light bulb. The reason for this was it allowed the minimum amount of light in order to deceive the attendee's, or am I just being cynical?

It does buy into the science and the electromagnetic field. The electromagnetic field is made up of three parts, magnetic, electrical charges and the light spectrum. In many ways this particular field causes the most speculation in the paranormal field. There are many reasons as to why the electromagnetic field fluctuates and spikes but this is another topic for another blog, in this instance we are talking about the light spectrum. Now bare in mind the word 'spectrum' in regards to light, this covers everything from Infrared – visible – ultraviolet. The visible light spectrum for humans is a meagre 1% of the entire spectrum, so by reducing this light into one frequency i.e red , it was considered something like tuning into a radio frequency and one that bridges the gap between realms. Apparently our white light makes it harder for spirit to manifest and one has to wonder if this may well be true. White light is made up of a rainbow of colours all resonating at different wavelengths so by restricting the wavelength to just one may be the way forward. Many famous physical medium experiments were done with restrictions of the light spectrum in place – The Scole Experiment, The Phillips experiment and even the Ganzfeld experiment – this has even moved forward in research as we found out when speaking with Dr Cal Cooper and his experiments with a floatation tank. Does the light spectrum affect our ability to be still and present allowing areas of our very own minds to achieve a hidden talent?

However just as many personal experiences and phenomena happen during the day which kind of blows the restricted light wavelength theory out of the water or does it? If we consider the kind of experiences that are happening and the intentions behind it then maybe this brings a whole new perspective. During the day many experiences happen by seemingly chance and this would include post/past death phenomena, precognition, apparition etc. The experience is not looked for it's just a question of wonder at what that could possibly have been, a glimpse into another realm perhaps. An unconsciously sort for experience. With the presence of the full light spectrum maybe the wavelengths are too confusing to be able to make sense of. To get into the correct frame of mind to experience maybe it's all to do with how busy your own brain is. So an experience during the day would possibly occur when you were at your most distracted by an emotion or a task, literally removed from the world around you, or actively seeking a connection with the other side through meditation or perhaps the concentration required by psychic mediums doing readings. Literally honing your own vibration to a limited strand. Many experiences have happened throughout the day that cannot be denied in many forms which leads us to ask does the light spectrum really matter.

One thing's for sure if the conditions are right then phenomena will happen, many groups sit for lengthy periods of time building up the right vibration frequency required to literally create or experience phenomena. Part of this process is the connection between the people involved and the strengthening of the energy between them. This is achieved through time, a common purpose and commitment. So maybe the question we need to ask ourselves if we need to achieve a certain state of resonance to experience phenomena then maybe we are actually the ones creating it and it's all just belief systems that we need to break down to achieve the impossible. Or, on the other side of the coin, maybe achieving that particular state of phenomena opens the door to endless possibilities.

In the spiritual field we talk about a spiritual form having a physical journey, that when we die we just change form, that energy can never die. So maybe, just maybe, all we do is change energetic form into a different frequency and somehow the constant physics of things like the electromagnetic field allows us a way to transcend the barriers and communicate or connect between?

Whatever the answer may be it one that needs a lot more thought!

Richard Clements
Parasearch Founder

Growing up in the 1970s and 80s Richard has always been drawn to the world of the unexplained, in an era before the internet and where paranormal related television programs were very few and far between Richard's main source of information gathering was in libraries. Although this alone would prove difficult as the number of books available on the subject was limited, this only added to the anticipation and excitement when a new book was added to the shelves of the very modestly stocked paranormal section. Ghosts, UFOs, Cryptids, and unsolved mysteries we're all fair game in his quest to satisfy a fascination with what might be lurking just out of sight in the world around him. During this time when the winter nights seemed longer and youngsters spent far more time outdoors with friends, night-time visits to the local churchyard always seemed to be a good idea and as a way of testing your nerve in front of your peers, added to this was a story of a ghost that was said to frequent the porch of the church. Whether this story was true or not was beside the point it had been doing the rounds of the school playground for years growing more ominous and dark with each retelling. It was against this backdrop that Richard first entered the little known and misunderstood world of the paranormal. Back in those early days interest in the paranormal is all you could really have, which was supplemented by occasional books and news articles. As with most things, Richards life continued first with leaving school, and entering the workplace starting a life working in the engineering industry, night-time visits to the graveyard seemed to be a thing of the past as the more important things became a concern visiting pubs and clubs and all the trappings that go with that. Although a fascination with the unexplained and paranormal never left him it certainly took a backseat ,but he would still make a point of watching the early TV shows like the Mysterious World of Arthur C Clarke, and a bit later Strange but True hosted by Michael Aspel which he still considers is the main foundation of his paranormal interest today. Running alongside Richard's interest at this time was an interest in military history which led to him being involved with a battle reenactment group called the English Civil War Society, between 1982 to 1995 Richard travelled extensively around the UK putting on displays for organisations such as English Heritage and the National Trust this not only gave him a good grounding and understanding of History but also put him in a very fortunate position of visiting and staying at a lot of historic sites up and down the country, whether Manor House, Castle or sites of historical significance. Although he will admit he never encountered anything he considered to be paranormal, the experience and the knowledge gained would stand him in good stead which he still relies upon today. When married life and family beckoned Richard and his then-wife moved to Australia in 1995, whilst living in Adelaide South Australia he became involved with the local UFO study group, which held monthly meetings and talks, it was during this period that his interest in the paranormal broadened to encompass ufology and cryptozoology. After returning back to the UK in 2005 and settling back in his home county of Essex, Richard felt there was still something missing in a way he could put to good use his interested in the paranormal. It wasn't till about 2015 he discovered podcasting and the amount of Paranormal content that was available through this broadcasting platform. Not an avid TV viewer, a lot of time was spent listening to podcasts and internet radio stations that

had a paranormal theme to them. It was in podcasting and radio that he saw the potential of expanding his interest in the paranormal in a more meaningful way. There were two particular radio stations at this time which Richard spent a lot of time listening to and interacting via their chat rooms during the live broadcasts which also gave the added advantage of getting to know and interact with the presenters. It was through this interaction and becoming friends that an opportunity arose when contacted by Paul Rook about an idea that Richard had had simmering in the back of his mind for some time. Due to circumstances, Paul was in a position to help and be involved in the idea that was to become Parasearch Radio. Starting in October 2016 and originally broadcast three nights a week, Parasearch Radio took its first tentative steps into the world of internet broadcasting. Like any new venture the early days we're a steep learning curve with all the drama and fun that any new station would face. Wanting to improve and move the station in the right direction Richard was very fortunate, with the help of Paul, when Kerry Greenaway joined the station which eventually would take Parasearch Radio to the next level by providing the benchmark in paranormal broadcasting. It was not long after Kerry, Richard recruited Penny G Morgan, which was to give Parasearch Radio a strong core foundation to build into the radio station you here today. Reflecting on life to date Richard has come to realise that maybe life's journey does serve a purpose with all its ups and downs along the way. There has always been one companion along his journey that has never left him and that has stayed loyal throughout, a companion he first encountered on the library shelves and in a small village graveyard in Essex back in the 1970s. Who's company has always been there. Although, this friend can be difficult to work out at times and sometimes leave you frustrated it has always left him with a sense of wonder and an inquiring mind into what might lie just out of sight. The companion in question is the paranormal!

Strange Encounter at Thetford Priory
By Richard Clements

Last Saturday (10/8/2019) myself and Paul Rook were in Norfolk exploring a couple of historic sites Paul has already written a blog about New Buckenham Castle, the first location we visited. After our visit, we moved on to the market town of Thetford and the ruins of its Priory. Thetford Priory is situated more or less on the outskirts of the town and is very accessible and is owned by English Heritage and free to enter, see the links for further details and history (https://www.english-heritage.org.uk/visit/places/thetford-priory/) (https://www.english-heritage.org.uk/visit/places/thetford-priory/history/).

It is not the purpose of this article to go into detail about the Priory in general as this can be found in the links above. I would, however, like to relate a strange tale that occurred back in August 1987 when a group of four teenagers was travelling through the town of Thetford on their way to a wargames meeting. When travelling through Thetford the group decided to stop off for a call of nature. Travelling down a side Street they came across the ruins of Thetford Priory, thinking the place was secluded enough they decided to answer nature's call with the help of the bush for added privacy.

At some point whilst heading back to the car they became aware of what appeared to be a figure observing them through an upper floor window of the ruined Priory. At first, they thought nothing of it until they noticed that now it was descending some stairs on the opposite side of a ground floor doorway. As the figure descended the stairs the group noticed it appeared to be wearing a black sheet or cloak of some description, not that dissimilar to a monks habit. The group then decided to go and investigate and upon approaching the doorway one of them decided to ascend the stairs towards the figure which they thought was somebody playing a practical joke. Upon getting about 2 steps up a flight of stairs the teenager hit his head against the flint masonry wall only to notice then but there was no staircase and no figure as well and this was observed by the remaining three of them. Immediately after this incident, the whole group were enveloped in what they said was a feeling of coldness and two of the group were actually physically sick.

It was at this point the realisation of the whole incident got the better of them and they decided to retreat at a rapid pace back to the car. What is strange though is as they were running back to the car the group got the sensation or the impression that the ruins of the Priory around them were somehow being rebuilt and also a sensation that they were running through what could only be described as quicksand that was slowing their progress up.

Not long after this event, the group had the foresight to write up their experiences individually. Although, the descriptions of the figure seen are not consistent through all the accounts, what is agreed upon is it was wearing some kind of black robe or cloak. The whole encountered did have a profound effect on the individuals who were involved, so much so that one member of the group became a writer and parapsychologist and the three others also decided to follow work in the scientific field.

This incident is interesting as it does appear to have some sort of crossover point between a traditional ghost sighting and a possible timeslip which have allegedly been experienced. One of the interesting points to note I feel is that timeslips if they do happen, and from the ones that have been reported always seem to occur to small groups of people, not individuals alone, food for thought perhaps?

Destination Framlingham Castle
Written By Richard Clements.

Our latest adventure took myself (Richard Clements), Kerry Greenaway, and Paul Rook over the county border into neighboring Suffolk to visit the historic town of Framlingham home to one of the UK's numerous castles.

Built just after the Norman conquest of England in 1066 by Roger Bigod, Earl of Norfolk, the castle was constructed to control and intimidate the local Anglo-Saxon populace in and around the area of Framlingham, which was considered a key strategic strongpoint. The original construction would have been of a wooden motte-and-bailey fortification typical of the time constructed between 1066 and 1107, it wasn't until after 1150 that a more permanent structure of stone buildings and fortifications were added.

During the reign of King Stephen (1135 - 1154), England was in complete chaos and civil unrest as the Barons started to seize control of castles across the country to use as their headquarters, this put the Barons in a very strong position seizing large areas of land and been able to control the local populations giving them the power to raise taxes independent of the crown, effectively becoming their own small kingdoms. It wasn't until after King Stephen's death it was left to the successor Henry II to regain control of the country, this he did by means of confiscating and taking back control of the lands lost by his predecessor. It was during this time that Framlingham

Castle was confiscated from the Bigod family, and remained in the King's possession until 1165 when it was purchased by Hugh Bigod a descendant of Roger Bigod for a large sum of money. The Bigod family, however, did not seem to learn their lesson and again rebelled against Henry II in 1173 and as a result, Hugh Bigod was sent into exile, and Henry II ordered Framlingham Castle to be dismantled which is a process known as slighting which is done to make a fortified position unserviceable and ineffective.

The Big On family regained Framlingham Castle back in 1189 during the reign of Richard I, it was at this time the curtain wall was constructed which still makes up the main part of the castle seen today. Roger Bigod II was one of the leading barons who forced King John to grant the Magna Carta. During the civil war which followed, King John successfully besieged and took control of Framlingham castle, but it was returned to the Bigod family when the civil war ended. Framlingham remained in the hands of the Bigod family until the fourteenth century when it passed to the Brotherton family, who were cousins of the king.

The Howard family inherited the castle in 1483 and set to work on a large-scale refurbishment project this is when Framlingham Castle ceased to be a fortified castle and more of a home. By the end of the sixteenth century, the castle had fallen into ruin.

It is to the backdrop of the brief history above we arrived at Framlingham Castle last Thursday afternoon (29/08/2000). To get to the castle you to wind your way through the small market town of Framlingham however, the Castle does not come into view to you're almost at the gate. As pointed out earlier the castle today consists of its curtain wall which is still mainly intact. Going through the main gate you are met by a large open green area which the curtain wall encompasses and to your left there are some buildings up against the main wall consisting of a Tudor Style house and some stone outbuildings which now contain a small museum, gift shop, and cafeteria.

Our first port of call was the take a walk around walkway surrounding the interior of the curtain wall. This involved going up a staircase that leads through the museum at one side of the Castle and then on to the walkway proper, from this vantage point as you walk around you had a good view of the hole interior grounds and good views across Framlingham and the surrounding countryside. We proceed at a slow pace which took us about 15 minutes to complete the circuit, Kerry, who freely admits she's not too good with heights managed really well. Descending the stairway at the far end of the walkway did prove to be a bit fraught for her, but escorted by her two knights in shining armor who came to the aid of the damsel in distress all ended happily ever after. We spent some time taking some photographs and then went outside to take a seat and get some refreshments. After this, myself and Kerry decided to take a walk around the whole of the exterior of the castle grounds. Framlingham Castle is as impressive on the outside as it is on the inside built the top a man-made mound and surrounded by defensive earthworks as you approach which involves a lot of up and down walking but well worth it when you come to the side of the castle which is bordered by a lake. It was here we decided to sit down and take in the view. Whilst we were chatting Kerry ask me about the possibility of tunnels leading away from the Castle, certainly, castles would have had cellars and perhaps rudimentary tunnels leading away I didn't really think much about what she said or why she said it, more about this later. We continued our walk in a clockwise direction around the remainder of the castle taking photographs along the way. We met back up with Paul inside the Castle and just sat back and chatted for about half-hour or so before making our way out and down into Framlingham for a late lunch in a nice pub just off the town square.

Ghostly goings-on reported.

The castle has several reports of Paranormal Activity, however, from what I was able to find out these are very rudimentary stories and not that dissimilar to any other historic building. which basically involve a lone staff member locking up at night and hearing or seeing something unusual. What has been heard are children playing in the empty courtyard this has been reported by both staff and members of the public. Faces of children peering through the upper floor windows, and footsteps on the gravel path leading through the main Gatehouse. Probably the most disturbing of all is disembodied screams that have been heard several times by staff members in the downstairs rooms.

I would now like to go back to the discussion me and Kerry had at the side of the Castle when she asked me about tunnels. It wasn't until later on that evening back at Kerry's that I asked her why she brought the subject up as it did seem unusual when she said it. Kerry had the feeling or intuition whatever you like to call it, that there was a tunnel leading away from the Castle. Castles, Manor Houses, and old monasteries are awash with stories of hidden tunnels and what I thought initially was what Kerry may have picked up on was nothing of any real weight. I decided whilst preparing this blog post to see if there were any stories about tunnels either at the Castle or around Framlingham itself, now there are no stories that really stuck out apart from one which is worth looking at.

As written about at the start of the article about the general history of Framlingham Castle, it had two points where it was involved in conflict the first been 1173 when the King ordered the confiscation of the castle and it's subsequent dismantling i.e.Slighting and again during the Baron Wars when it was laid siege to by King John. The first process mention of slighting is to prevent a strong point been reused this would involve work knocking down exterior walls and wakening the general structure of the fortification. The most common method back in the Middle Ages to either bring down of castle wall or to weaken it sufficiently was to dig a tunnel from outside of the defenses to directly under the part of the wall or Tower you wish to weaken or bring down, you would sink a tunnel and then build a large chamber underneath the wall propped up with wouldn't joists you would then pack the chamber with combustible material and set light to it and hopefully the heat generated would be sufficient to crack and bring down part of the wall or to severely weaken it. Both these processes would have been used during the time Framlingham Castle was slighted and during the Siege to gain entry, and have been recorded in documentation.

Although it wasn't really our purpose to visit Framlingham for a paranormal experience the castle does offer a great day out regardless with wide-open spaces both inside and out to explore and to kick back and relax with a unique and historic setting as a backdrop. The castle is an English Heritage property and can be looked up via their website which will give you all the information you need to visit whether you are relatively local or from further afield traveling by, we would say you won't be disappointed spending some time Framlingham Castle.

Bromham Mill Charity Ghost Hunt
Written By Richard Clements

On Friday (06/09/2019) Parasearch Radio was invited to attend a charity event to help raise money for people that suffer from a rare condition known as lipodystrophy, a genetic disorder that affects about 700 people in the UK, in which the body is unable to produce and maintain healthy fat tissue. The event was hosted by The Paranormal Charity Warriors, a group that Parasearch Radio is proud to be associated with and support. The event took the form of a public paranormal investigation night held at Bromham Mill, Bedford which is owned and operated by Bedford County Council, the Mill is now a tourist attraction housing the restored water Mill workings, cafeteria, Craft Centre, and workshop.

The Paranormal Charity Warriors very kindly offered Parasearch Radio, to allow three of us to attend the event as special guests for the evening and to help assist the group with the investigation of the Mill. It was decided that the most special of the people involved in the station would attend and naturally without any argument this was myself (Richard Clements) station founder, Paul Rook, joint owner and presenter, and our very own Alien Guy from the Dark Mirror Paranormal Show, presenter Mark Manley.

Myself and Paul travel up from Essex during the afternoon to meet up with the team for a pre investigation get together and dinner at a local carvery, this gave me and Paul a chance to meet and get to know the guys and girls of the Paranormal Charity Warriors. We were made to feel very welcome and we both enjoyed the food and company and it was a good jumping-off point to go onto the event.

That has been a Watermill at Bromham from as far back as 1089 this is known by an entry in the Domesday Book compiled in that year. The buildings that make up Bromham Mill as it stands today was constructed in and around the late 18th and early 19th centuries and are built using the local stone. There is the main building which is the Watermill proper and a house that was originally the Millers house which is opposite the main Mill building across the courtyard. We arrived at about 6:30 in the evening and set about the usual pre-investigation work of unloading cars and setting up the inside ready for the public when they arrived. Myself and Paul took this opportunity to walk around and familiarise ourselves with the location, and whilst there was still daylight I went off to take interior and exterior photos of the whole location and posted a gallery of photos to the Paraseach Radio facebook page.

It was around 8 pm that the paying guests started to arrive and also so our very own Mark Manley who done very well getting down from Yorkshire to attend the event, and also the two other special guests Sara and Phil Whyman who had travelled equally as far and managed to fight against the Friday evening traffic. The start of the evening was an introduction from the team, demonstrations, and explanations of some of the equipment that will be used during the night. We were then split into 3 groups, myself, Mark, and Jay Austin of the Paranormal Charity Warriors lead one group, and Paul was with Sara and Phil Whyman, and Dan Litchfield of The Paranormal Charity Warriors in another group. Myself and Marks group were assigned the Mill whereas Paul's group went over to the Miller's house which was their location for the evening, and there was a third group that was assigned an outside area down by the river. Jay, myself, and Mark took our group through into the Mill area for a general walkthrough and to see whether anyone in the group could pick up on anything, Mark had set up a few of his experiments along the way that were left to run throughout the evening. The group did a few callouts to see if we could get a response on some of the equipment without success. I had my dowsing rods with me and these did respond very well to the questions being asked which were basics yes, no answer questions, so we worked that way throughout the first Group session managing to come up with some interesting information regarding the name of Robert or Bob who seemed to have come traveled up from Suffolk, for work and was a Carter for the mill around the year 1830.

The night progressed really well along pretty much the sorts of experiences that happened above and form what I can gather the other groups reporting similar activity not so much any physical or visual activity but more of a subtle nature through the more spiritual old fashioned techniques. We stayed in our locations whilst the public was rotated through the three locations. This was broken up with breaks in between for tea and coffee and what seemed an awful lot of delicious cake.

Around 1 am and all the groups had visited each area around the location to do their visuals and experiments we had our final break of the evening before all gathering back upstairs in the main hub for a transfiguration session with team medium Sam Bennett. Two people had already volunteered to work with Sam through this process, to be honest, I have never witnessed or known much about the practice of the transfiguration. The first person who volunteered was a member of the public on the event who was a sceptic. Sam explained the process to everyone and what to look out for if anything should happen, the volunteer sat in the chair and the lights were dimmed and a torch put up to his face. Sam then proceeded to talk to the person and appear to guide him through and meditation process from my experience known as a body scan, which involves relaxing your entire body from your feet upwards in stages. Whilst he was going through this process he was encouraged to speak out aloud any thoughts or images that were coming into his head and we were told to focus on his facial expressions to see whether they were changing and if so to say so as well. Although the volunteer came back with nothing of any substance there did seem to be a general consensus there was a slight altering around his eyes during this process which I must admit I did notice as well. Next, up in the hot seat was our very own Mark Manley, Sam repeated the same process as before talking Mark through a meditative process whilst at the same time encouraging him to talk and describe what he was seeing or feeling. Unlike the first person, Mark did go into quite some detail of what he was seeing and sensing again we were asked to look at his facial expressions to see if they were changing, this did not appear to happen, he didn't even transfigure into the alien that we were all anticipating!

This more or less brought a close to the evening's events, we moved on to the raffle draw which the girls had been hard at work selling tickets all evening for. At the end of the event it was announced that the total raised throughout the evening was an impressive amount of £1,222. I would like to say from myself, Mark, Paul who attended and everyone else from Parasearch Radio a big thank you and well-done for letting us be involved and with your great work and long may it continue. Parasearch Radio would like to thank The Paranormal Charity Warriors for a great evening, who are, Lisa Gardner, Sam Bennetts, Joanne Treherne, Lucy Day, Ness Watts, Caroline Sherman Thomas, Jay Austin, Dan Litchfield, and Matt Leavey.

For further information of that coming events please visit their website https://www.paranormalsisters-charitywarriors.co.uk/

One week, One Priory, One Abbey
Written By Richard Clements

When out and about it's always worth keeping an eye out for places of interest you may be able to pay an impromptu visit whilst going about your daily business. One such opportunity arose the other day when I was out shopping in Colchester, Essex, I saw a sign pointing towards the ruins of St Botolph's Priory. I've known about the ruins for some time now but what with one thing or another have never taken time out to go and visit but as I was considering getting lunch I thought what better opportunity to have something to eat and then and go and explore, and I was glad I did.

St Botolph's Priory is located by the southern gateway through Colchester's old town walls, founded around the year 1100 the Priory was the first Augustinian monastery in Britain and stands in the heart of modern-day Colchester. Dedicated to St Julian and St Botolph, the Priory was dissolved by Henry VIII in 1536, and left to fall into disrepair, further destruction was inflicted during the 1648 siege of Colchester during the English Civil War, you can still see the damage caused by cannon fire during the siege, and what remains of the Priory today is pretty much how it was left at the end of the siege.

What remains today is the nave of the Priory, although, in a ruined state I still got a good impression of what the structure would have looked like in its original state and with a bit of imagination thrown into the mix, it is basically just missing its roof and a couple of interior walls. You can clearly see that most of the building was built from flint and recycled Roman bricks from in and around Colchester, the main decorative stone for the arches and doorways was imported from France. From the inside facing the entrance to your right is probably the most impressive feature of the ruin, a double layer of Norman archers that still stand to their full height and give you a good idea of how large a covered building St Botolph's would have been. Walking through the arches brings you back to the outside of the Priory and the small graveyard that is on the west side of the building. Many people myself included have often wondered why the ruins of St Botolph's are not better known and visited as it is regarded to be the best example of a 12th-century Priory in the country and probably the most easily accessible.

Surprisingly, there does not seem to be much written about paranormal activity in or around the Priory, however, I did come across one brief story from the Haunted Rooms website which is worth quoting. " In 1993 a young local girl was playing in the ruins with her friends when she suddenly spotted a dark figure standing next to one of the tombs watching her and her friends. She was understandably startled but said that the figure simply smiled at her and then vanished into thin air right in front of her eyes. There have been a handful of similar accounts over the years."

If you wish to visit, the Priory ruins are on Priory Street, at the bottom of Queen Street, only a short distance from Colchester tourist information centre and castle.

A couple of days later saw me venturing out again only this time with Paul Rook who wanted to show me the area where he grew up in and around the London borough of Bexley in Kent, and the ruins of Lesnes Abbey.

The ruins of Lesnes Abbey stand near the south bank of the River Thames, on the eastern fringes of suburban London. The Abbey was founded by Richard de Luci, Chief Justiciar of England to Henry II in 1178, it is said he had it constructed as penance for his involvement in the murder of the Archbishop of Canterbury Thomas Becket in 1170.

From the guilty conscience that gave rise to its construction, the Abbey never grew to any great size compared to other monastic buildings constructed around the same time. However, the Abbey was the first to get the attention in 1525 from Cardinal Wolsey, working on behalf of Henry VIII, and holds the prestigious title of being the first monastery of the dissolution that was to follow. The monastic buildings were destroyed except for the Abbot's own lodging, which served as a mansion for the manor of Lesnes. The rest of the site was robbed for building materials and the abbot's house was turned into a farmhouse.

When we arrived the Abbey sits atop a small rise just off the main road (Abbey Road, Bexley) and is easily accessible. Even though it's considered a small site I was quite surprised just how large it actually was. Although, there are walls and doorways surrounding part of the Abbey which reach about 9 ft in height, what is left is basically a low lying floor plan. It was as we were walking around Paul pointed out an altar area that archaeologists had unearthed a casket containing the remains of a human heart, from what I've managed to find out is that this was quite a common practice in medieval times for high ranking nobles to have their hearts placed after death beneath the altars of churches and monasteries. We spent about an hour exploring the site that allowed me to take plenty of photographs that I posted up in a gallery on the Parasearch Radio Facebook page.

Paul has investigated Lernes back in the early days of his paranormal career as part of a group investigation and was saying that they did have some interesting results on the equipment used. However, I did manage to come across a couple of stories connected to the Abbey. There is a story of a horseman spotted in the abbey grounds as recently as 2013 that was seen by a lady who was conducting a walking tour around the ruins. In a newspaper article, she said she first heard about the horseman, clad in a tunic and leggings, appearing in a photo taken by her grandfather in the 1930s. The newspaper article was accompanied by the said photograph and to be quite honest I couldn't really see anything of note in it. The second story is a more traditional ghostly tale associated with a lot of monasteries involving an amorous relationship between a monk and one of the local women, which was to end in tragedy when they were found out by the Abbot who had the monk put to death for his indiscretion, and it is said he can be seen wandering the woods behind the Abbey to this day.

Like St Botolph's Priory, Lesnes Abbey grounds are open to the public at any time. However, please remember if you do plan to visit especially during the Night-Time hours please show respect and act responsibly, these are historic monuments for everyone to enjoy both night and day.

Beacon Hill Fort
Written by Richard Clements

Beacon Hill Fort in Harwich, Essex, is an ex-military gun battery that was conceived and built in the late 1800s and substantially redesigned and added on to during both world wars to defend the ports of Harwich, and Felixstowe, against the threat of naval seaborne invasion. Located a stone's throw from the older Harbour Defence of Harwich Redoubt that was completed during the Napoleonic Wars in 1810 but by the 1880s, was considered outdated and obsolete with the rapid advancement and effectiveness of coastal artillery throughout this period of 19th century, it was decided a new harbor defense was needed, so in 1889 work began on a new gun battery, which was completed in 1892 that has become known today as Beacon Hill Fort.

So with this brief history in mind, it was decided that a Parasearch Radio road trip by myself, Paul Rook with the company of Lucy Albrighton of Phoenix Paranormal Midlands, should head over to Harwich and explore this little known about location, and we were not to be disappointed.

For those of you familiar with Harwich Redoubt, as mentioned above, Beacon Hill Fort is only situated about 200 yards away on the same housing estate and sits right on the foreshore of the Harbour. Open to visitors Saturdays and Sundays from 10 a.m. to 4 p.m. throughout the winter months and free admission, we were welcomed and giving a brief history of the fort along with a map and a written guide and then were left to explore the whole site by ourselves. The word fort is a bit misleading as in reality it is what is known as a gun battery there are various gun emplacements along the top of the harbor breakwater that are all independent of each other with their ammunition magazines situated directly beneath each gun and barrack block for the crew.

The fortified gun emplacements of which there are three main guns which are supported by two lighter gun batteries are situated in a straight line along the foreshore facing outwards towards the sea. The ground level of these batteries you can see are of first world war vintage whereas the structures now covering them are more than likely to be World War Two add-ons erected over the original casings for extra armament and protection. On the left-hand flank of the gun battery as you face it from the rear there is the fire control and ranging tower. This is a three-story building that is still accessible, this would have been used by personnel using range-finding telescopes to work out the exact distance of enemy vessels and to relay all relevant information to the gun crews so as they could range the guns to the correct distance and direction of any enemy threat. Although the original gun positions are minus their guns and all the equipment they would have had installed you still get a good idea of what it may have been like during its operational service up until the mid-1950s when the site was decommissioned.

To the rear of the main gun batteries separated by a trackway lie all the service and support buildings i.e an electricity-generating block, storage facilities, and other essential outbuildings that would have serviced the Garrison stationed there during times of war.

And there's more! Above-ground what we have been exploring was a mixture of buildings and gun emplacements dating from about 1914 through to the 1940s. However, a lot of the structure is underground and these are the oldest part of the Fort that dates back to its original construction in the 1890s, these are also open to the public, upon admission to the site you are also given a torch/flashlight for you to explore these places as well. The brick-lined underground galleries would have been areas where the shells and the explosive propellants for the guns would have been stored directly beneath the batteries and fed up to the gun crews above as and when required. These areas are by far the most atmospheric places to visit whilst exploring the Fort.

I can highly recommend a visit Beacon Hill Fort, volunteers who maintain the Fort are approachable and a wealth of information and are more than willing to have a chat and answer any questions you have whilst exploring this little known gem of a location, for more information and to plan your day out go to https://www.beaconhillfort.org.uk/

Mark Manley
Co Host of The Dark Mirror Show

Mark Manley. co-hosts The Dark Mirrorshow with Kerry Greenaway. He is a 4th Dan kickboxing instructor, and is also a Manager with Phoenix Paranormal Ltd. He is also a long suffering dad of 2

teenage daughters, and now a proud grandfather. The reason he is losing his hair is because he is a father of 2 girls and a co host with Kerry Greenaway and Carl Hutchinson. "I love doing the Dark mirror show", I love all the research, the subjects, my co-host, and shouting my catchphrase "ALIENS" extremely loudly, much to the chagrin of Kerry. My job is complete if I get her to burst out
Laughing"

Bigfoot, sasquatch, yeti, hairy men, yowie, orang-pendek.
Written by Mark Manley

Now, as you know, I'm normally the "ALIENS" guy. But sometimes, just sometimes,

I do like to talk about other things, and no, I don't mean myself.

So this time, this blog will be about all the different types of Bigfoot.....

Or Gigantopithecus as it may be known.

Now, there are many many sightings all over the world of varying types of Bigfoot,

From Canada, all the way to Australia, whilst crossing North America, Hawaii where they have the "Menehune", Scotland with reports of the "hairy men" way up in the mountains, most of Europe, Asia, even during the Vietnam war, and the former Soviet Union where they are known as the "Almas".

Whilst the most popular sightings seem to be in North America, there are increasingly more and more sightings in eastern Europe, and especially the Russian continent, with the latest

Sighting being in the Russian city of Severodvinsk on February 18th this year, there is also some grainy dashcam footage of the sighting, there is also an interesting video that schoolboy Yevgeny Anisimov aged 11, and 2 of his friends, were 30km from the city of Leninsk-Kuznetsky in Kemerovo region, playing in the snow when they noticed a chain of huge tracks in the snow.

They got very inquisitive about the tracks and followed the trail, filming them on the mobile phone camera.

They followed the tracks for a bit and got closer to the bushes - where suddenly they saw a Yeti, some 50 metres away from them.

It noticed them as well, sharply moved, bent down, then to the left, and ran left. The boys, scared, ran in the opposite direction.

Yevgeny, who is filming the 'creature' - is heard shouting " I'm the nearest, I'm going to be eaten".

Now, I'm not saying that every single sighting, picture, video, noise, or knocking heard is a

Bigfoot.

But I am saying that I truly believe that there are these creatures all over the world.

I mean, if you think about it, why wouldn't there be?

There are more and more new species being discovered every day all over the world.

There are species once thought extinct, being found as well.
So here's my theory on this, bare with me as I get my thinking head out of the fridge.

Now, the earth was once 1 giant supercontinent called "Pangia", all before the continent's broke up, and some slipped under the waves, and we ended up the continent's and land mass as we know it now.
When it was all joined together, we had great apes all over it like Gigantopithecus etc.

Now these great apes migrated and spread to all corners of the supercontinent.

Stay with me on this.

So, if you have all these great apes, all over the supercontinent, then they were still there when the supercontinent broke up into the land we now know.

So that means that there would have been great numbers of these hairy guys (probably related to me) all over the place, and pretty much now, on every single new continent.

Now if pockets of these guys survived, as I think they did, then because they would be on all parts of these new continent's, then maybe that would explain 2 things.

A, why you have sightings, because some survived, and

B, this is why you have sightings all over the world including the "Yowies" in Australia, because they had spread all over Pangia, before it broke up.
Now I have heard some very very "out there" theories of why we have Bigfoot, including "earth is actually a

prison planet, and they are intergalactic prisoners sent here"!

I may be the "Aliens" guy, but even I can't go along with that one!
I think there may very well be a lot of "Cryptid" sightings, that all stem from pockets of various creatures migrating just like Bigfoot did, and I think we may still have many more to find.

Now I'm going to take my dried frog pills and have a lie down.

Let me know what you think, and remember..........ALIENS!!!

Tattoos + Haunted - Madness.
Written by Mark Manley.

We recently did a show on tattoo's, and the notion of whether they could be haunted

At any time or not.

Well, personally I think it depends on your beliefs, culture, religion etc.

So I'll give you a bit of the history and background of tattoo's, some of the omens, and some of the tales of which tattoo is bad luck to have etc, that way my dear reader, you can make your own mind up about tattoos.

Tattoo's go back to ancient Egyptian times, and further back still.

The oldest tattoo on record is that of Otzi the iceman, and no, he isn't a burly ex navy sea dog, who now drives around in a little ice cream van selling 99's to unsuspecting passers by. Otzi the iceman, was found in the Otzal Alps in September of 1991, hence his nickname "Otzi", his body had been perfectly preserved in ice in the glaciers there, and as they started to melt, his body was revealed.

Otzi has 61 tattoos, and the majority of these are inscriptions on his legs, interestingly, there was not really any ink way back then, so the tattoo's were analysed, and found to be a mixture of soot and fireplace ash.....now I have quite a few tattoos, most of them Chinese, mythical, and very colourful, but I think if my tattooist was going to say to me "today, were going to try something different" and came in waving half a bbq at me, I'd probably swear and run away!

But, it just goes to show you the ingenuity there was back then, I mean, nearly 3 and a half millennia before JC popped into the world, and tribes were marking there people up with various tattoos to indicate there status,job, and where they were from, incidentally, Otzi died from an arrow to the knee......he must have been an adventurer! (It was an arrow in his back silly)

Now, there is evidence of tattoo's from over 49 different places around the world, going from as far up as Alaska, as far south as the Minoans, and as far east as Russia ,Mongolia etc.

Even in the Far East, they have evidence of tattoo's having been done from around 2100 BC, and these days, Chinese, Japanese, and Viking tattoos are the most popular.

Now in china all those years ago, tattoos were frowned upon ...bit like my poor old mum and my tattoo's, when I pop down for a visit, if I've got a new tattoo, she rolls her eyes and gives me that "knowing" look that all mums can do.

In ancient China, tattoos were the things that heroes and bandits wore, yet in ancient Egypt, they were predominantly only for women, and they were for the purpose of covering scars, putting healing spells and prayers on operation sites, and also purely for cosmetic purposes.

Hop back to china, and come forward to around the 16th century, and you will find the Dulong people, who settled along the Dulong river in nomadic groups, now these poor people, used to get raided by bandits, and other tribes, and the women were either taken as slaves, or concubines, either way, not nice, so they decided that if they had tattoos on their faces, then they wouldn't be very attractive to the people who raided them, so that's just what they did, and it actually worked. The women weren't taken away anymore, nowadays, they still practice the facial tattooing, but these days it is a right of passage for teenage girls, and they receive their first tattoo at the ripe old age of 12, or 13.

Now the Dai people of China (and not Wales) also have a tattooing heritage that goes back hundreds of years, in ancient times they would tattoo their children as young as 5 or 6, but nowadays it's the same as the Dulong people and it's a right of passage at 14 or 15, the tattoo's there however are to signify strength and virility, so you'll normally see dragons or tigers.

Now, over here in the west, I strongly advise that you think long and hard about what tattoo you want to have, were not nomadic tribes now, so going to Ibiza and coming back with a highly "Adult" tattoo, does not make you a warrior or provider, it makes you a t""t who has some explaining to do to his mum and partner.

Now, a lot of tattoos are powerful, they come from legend, and are symbols in spirituality, lore, or status. Take the dragon, I have several, but each one represents things like, luck, strength, longevity etc (but not the Spiro one), did you know there is a long held belief that when you have a dragon tattoo done, you must always have the eyes done last, as they are the windows to the soul of not just a dragon, but you as well, my latest dragon is almost finished, but the eyes have yet to be finished.

Now, here are a few myths and dos and don'ts of tattoo lore.

Never, and I really do mean NEVER, get your other halves name tattooed on you, anywhere, and yes im including on that too, because as soon as you do, that's it, it's like putting bad juju or a hex on your relationship, most tattooists that put the name on you, will see you back in the next few months to cover it up.

Another bad one is having a cross done, because if it's on your arms, it always appears upside down to other people, and the last thing you want is flying nuns chasing you down the road screaming "heretic" at you and startling the neighbours.

The same goes with having 3 6's tattooed on you...I mean really, it speaks for itself that one.

A lot of runes and sigils that you see around these days, normally on hipsters in jeans with turn ups and man buns, actually have a much deeper esoteric meaning, originally

Made and used as a bridge in the gap between the conscious and subconscious mind, so whilst your sipping your pims in central London, showing off your new beard and matching tattoos to all your fellow turn up wearing friends, who incidentally have

similar tattoo's, there's a white witch looking at it going "he needs to what his what"???......not cool.

Dark tattoos, while there's not really a lot of folklore surrounding these, having Freddie Kruger or Jason, or even Cudjo tattooed on you, may look cool, but remember when you're older, you will have to look your 4 year old granddaughter in the eye and explain yourself to them, and trust me, they will not let up till they are satisfied with your answer.

Now tattoo's these days, although they do have a certain stigma still attached to them, are in vogue and can be very cool, although personally I would never have them done on my hands or neck as I think it's scruffy, but that is only my own opinion.

As far as can tattoos be haunted,...I don't think so, I mean yes, the tattoo artist, is putting their own energy into the actual making of the tattoo, and a lot of people these days, are having a bit of ash from a passed loved one or pet, added to the ink, and although I think that's actually quite a beautiful and loving thing to do, I don't however think it makes the tattoo haunted.

In all my research and years of investigating the paranormal, I have never come across any tales or evidence of tattoo's being haunted.

I did however find this 1, and I really do mean 1 story.

It involved and ancient Japanese shoguns personal tattooist and physician. I couldn't find any names, or a time period for it, but apparently the tattoo's were done by the ancient "stick and poke" technique, anyway, a feuding rival shogun, decided that this guys tattoo's were the best in all Japan, so he tried to bribe the tattooist with unparalleled riches to leave his master, and defect to him. This did not work, he tried having him kidnapped, that didn't work, so in the end, he sent out some of his personal guard to kill him, now when they got to the castle, they silently entered, and started killing the guards and look outs, and the further they penetrated the castles defences, the more there number was whittled down, eventually, only one of the shoguns personal guards managed to enter the chambers of the tattooist, the tattooist was only slight, and was an old man, he tried in vain to protect himself, but unfortunately died after having a dagger thrust into his heart, the old man did however manage to pierce his attackers skin with the needle from his stick and poke, and as he lay dying on the floor, cursed his attacker, to be transformed into a living tattoo, unable to ever be able to get rid of the tattoo.

When he died, the attacker took his mask off, it was the rival shogun.

He spat on the old man's body and fled back to his castle.

Now over the next few days, he noticed a scratch on his arm that was getting itchy, and the more he scratched it, the more it darkens and the more it spreads, eventually covering his entire body and extremities, it started to climb towards his face, he called in his personal doctor, and his priests, he was asked if he was the one who killed the old tattooist because they thought it looked like a curse, he shouted at them and had them executed, eventually, the tattoo covered him entirely, head to foot, there was not one inch of his skin uncovered. Now, he lost his followers faith in him, his

power as a shogun was dissipating, his generals left him when they heard it was him who killed the old tattooist and then anyone who accused him of it, to his wife, he begged and pleaded with her not to leave him, and she did, telling him she knew what he had done.

He decided to end it all and commit seppuku, but, he decided to do it in his bath house, and so, he went into his bath house, knelt in the water, and disembowels himself, and as he rolled over, he managed to pull himself into the corner of the bath and prop himself up.

As he watched his life slowly drain away, and change the water to red, he noticed a highly polished brass mirror in front of him ...and the last thing he saw before his last breath left him, was the chest piece of his cursed tattoo, the chest piece, depicted a little old

Chinese man being slain by an attacker, and this attackers mask was off, and the face he saw in that tattoo of the attacker, was his own face, looking back at him, and grinning..........good night kiddies.

https://www.spreaker.com/user/parasearchuk/the-dark-mirror-show-can-tattoos-be-haun_1

Sam Mason
Co Host of the PSH Radio Show

Sam Mason has a keen interest in the paranormal and has the inherited ability to see spirit. This peeked when she first started watching paranormal TV shows and she decided to go on a public ghost hunt with a local team at the local town hall. She continued to watch paranormal TV shows and that is when she decided to set up PSH Radio so she could interview people who have the same interest in the paranormal as her.

When she started doing paranormal investigating she had a few tech items but in late 2018 she decided to scrap the tech and just keep her night vision camcorder. Now she uses her own feelings and senses on investigations. She has been to so many haunted locations she has lost count. In October 2019 she had the opportunity to do a short spirit box session as the Tonopah Graveyard in Tonopah NV this also included visiting the famous Clown Motel.

She appeared in her first ever Youtube series "Paranormal Voyages-The Clown Motel" which of course includes the part she did at the Tonopah Graveyard. As she continues to go on her paranormal journey she is beginning to learn more about how to use her own senses & feelings to use on Paranormal Investigations.

Zak Bagans Museum Tour
Written by Sam Mason

This museum is a little different and if you know who Zak Bagans is then you will know why. I am not just talking about the items that are in place, but the building itself. If you live in Vegas and have maybe driven past the museum or even seen photos online you would think it was a tiny building but in fact there are over 30 rooms with different items inside them. Even when you go to the lobby where you purchase your ticket and meet your first tour guide there are items. It is hard to explain how the building inside looks unless you have been there yourself, yes there is photos online but they do not do it justice at all. It's kind of like a haunted house type theme, some of the corridors have exposed looking wood slabs with red lights in them which makes it look super cool.

In this blog I am not going to mention every single room in the museum, I am just going to talk about the room's I went into because for the first time ever I did not go into all of the rooms but that will be explained further on!

So I am going to start this off by saying that in all the years I have been involved in the paranormal field this is the first time I felt how I did, my friends who know me know that I usually just brush experiences off and just forget about them but not this time, this is going to stick with me for a very long time and I have so many questions which no doubt will be left unanswered. As you read this you can of course make your own mind up of what actually happened to me. So I am just going to start this off by saying I have visited the museum a few times now and I have never once felt anxious about going there, yes I have been nervous but not anxious. The first time I was there was last year so that is understandable as I had no idea what to expect, but this time it was different. It is hard to explain how I felt because it's my feelings and my body but I hope this blog will give you some understanding.

As soon as I stepped into the first room of the museum I felt on edge I was unable to concentrate, as the tour guide was talking I was looking around the room and I turned to face the back of the room where the Zak Zoltar is. They have a few items on the walls and at the area where they had told us a painting has fallen off the wall since they added "Gretchen" into the room I saw a brief shadow of a person dash across the back wall. I turned around then I saw a full blown person walk past the big open doorway which leads into the open area as you come in, not sure if the staff use that door when tours are going on or not so that is unanswered at this moment.

The next room I started to experience things in housed the Bella Lugosi Mirror. A few moments after the tour guide moved the curtain from the mirror so some people in the tour could peer into the mirror, the right side of my lower back started to burn. I just stood there waiting, thinking it could just be the heat. As the tour went on we went into the Dr Kevorkian's Van room, I said nothing for a short while until one of my friends asked if I was ok as she saw I was troubled. I told her that part of my back had been burning since the room with the mirror. The tour guide asked if I had been scratched and I replied I think so, he said he was unable to check as he had left his torch in the break room. My friends tried to look but of course with lighting it was a struggle so we waited until we were able to see it properly.

The first room I refused to go into was the Dybbuk box room my gut feeling was telling me not too, it's hard to explain this feeling and my back was becoming increasingly uncomfortable. The next room I went into was the Devils rocking chair room. My back was continuing to burn and it felt like someone was digging their nails and clawing at this area. The tour guide asked if I was ok and I pulled my top up slightly so she could look at where the burning was, she said there were swelt lines but no red scratches as of yet. After this I refused to go into any of the rooms where I had that gut feeling of something about to happen.

As we waited to enter the gift shop I started to rock and nearly ended up falling back. I know doing what I do this is how I react when spirits are taking my energy. Once we had entered the gift shop my friends were able to look properly at the right side of my back and sure enough scratches had appeared I got asked the usual questions, Are you sure you did not scratch your back, handbag position, clothes creases etc but I couldn't offer an explanation. This ended my first visit on this vacation but I was set to return!

The Return

Our second visit to the museum was a few days later and I felt much better than I had the previous visit. I was eager and excited to do the tour again I wanted to experience the whole museum even the rooms I missed last time.

The first room I felt off in was the Dr Kevorkian office this is the room you are in before one of the group opens the door to the van room. In this room the light gets switched off so you can watch two short videos one of cctv and one of Zak. I did not take notice in this room at all and I kept looking back at the light up cabinet which they have in the office and to me the lights kept going on and off. I have no idea if anyone kept blocking the light out, I just kept getting the urge to look back, there was a biggish gap between myself and some other members of the public. I saw this massive shadow which was taller than the two other people who stood with me in this room. They show you a cctv clip of two females who freaked out as one of them saw a creepy shadow person behind one of the staff members (I can't remember the full video explanation) so did I really see this shadow figure or was it psychological suggestion? Who knows! My friend Leslie volunteered to open the door to the next room and as we both stepped in we felt a huge heavy energy in there. I needed to go and sit down straight away I could not wait to get out of that room.

When we entered the Celebrity room, I felt instantly sick this is one of the rooms that had never affected me before. At this point I could have easily called it quits and finished the tour but I rationalized this feeling and put it down to just nerves or something.

The last room we entered was the fun house room, this is where John Shaw does his sideshow performance. Leslie was at the front and urged me to join her however although I was reluctant, with her reassurance I moved to join her. As soon as I reached the front John started to talk. The room is also filled with a lot more items and I was drawn to a mini animatronics figure in front of me. I became fixated with this item and it felt like we were having a staring match. I was moving my head and eyes wanting to check it out more and I felt something was looking back at me through this item. I broke its gaze and returned to listening to John at this point the feeling of claustrophobia and the need to escape overwhelmed me, it felt like the walls were closing in on me. I got asked if this was a panic attack but I have had panic attacks/ anxiety attacks before and this was not the same. I was on the point of tears and looked at my friend saying "I can't do this anymore I need to get out" she immediately took action and enveloped me in a hug hold whilst looking for the exit or a tour guide. Emotion over came me and everything became blurred. I finally came to my senses after seeing the clown who jumps out on people, well that's enough to bring anyone to their senses! All I wanted to do was to get out of the building, I was shaking but I wasn't cold and the feeling of claustrophobia was still upon me. John let myself and my friend out of the building and as soon as I stepped foot outside the building I nearly passed out.

On the way back to the hotel I was shivering in the car and felt drained of energy, remember I'm in Vegas so it's impossible to be cold and I still felt that something was with me. I drew up my protections and ordered it to return to the Museum. As soon as I reached the hotel I had to rush to the restroom to vomit, was it just after the shock of the experience

Having read my account of my own experiences at the museum I leave you to make up your own mind. However all I will say is that if you can sense energy then you will feel it as soon as you hit the parking lot. Whatever you make of my experiences one thing's for sure, Zac Baggans – The Haunted Museum is definitely worth a visit.

Penny G Morgan
Host of Haunted Histories

Penny has had an interest in all things unusual since a young age after experiencing seeing a light anomaly in an old barn in the village that she grew up in.

Her love of history has led her to visit as many museums, old buildings and ruins that was humanly possible and fast forward some years and she was given the chance to embrace both her love by presenting Haunted Histories for Parasearch Radio on www.spreaker.com/user/parasearchuk

at 9pm UK every Wednesday. A show where she has got to talk investigating and history with pretty much anyone who is anyone in the paranormal world including people like Lee Roberts, Chris Smith of Tennessee Wraith Chasers, writer Richard Estep and the Lacey to her Cagney, Jayne Harris.

November 2018 gave her the opportunity to be the roving reporter, getting to interview both the guests and attendees at Sage Paracon, proving even further her ability to be able to create a conversation out of thin air.

She was also featured in a women in the paranormal article for the Daily Mail at the beginning of 2019, and also writes a regular feature for Haunted Magazine called "Not so 'orrible histories", has appeared on Paul Ross' radio show and was even a special guest at the October 2019 Usborne book launch for Ghosts.

If that was not enough, she is also a published author, her first book "My Haunted History" is available on Amazon and her new book, "A Haunted Experiment" will be available in early 2020.

Somehow she also finds time to be a wife, mum of two young boys, lift weights at the gym and belt out the odd hard rock classic when opportunity allows – it's true what they say, if you want something done, give it to a busy person.

The Angels of Mons
Written by Penny G Morgan

It is hard to cover every single aspect of this "legend" without leaving out details that someone may feel is critical in only 500 words, I'm sure students of history get to convey their knowledge and understanding of the situation in thousands of words so if I have omitted something that you think is obvious, I apologise in advance.

The Angels of Mons are one of the most famous supernatural stories associated with World War One, although it is not the only account of celestial intervention that has been recorded in some form or another. When you think of abject horror and destruction these young men were experiencing – and the women just slightly back from the front line in medical and voluntary roles – it is not surprising that some turned to divine intervention to make it through.

The Battle of Mons was seen to be the first major action seen by the British Expeditionary Forces of WW1 and took place on the 22nd and 23rd August in 1914, this is probably where historians will criticise me for skimming over the details of this offensive but in a nutshell, the Commonwealth forces numbered around 4,000 men, whilst the Germ 1st Army which was approaching from the east had around 21,000. Hence a retreat was ordered, as anyone who studies history and especially historical warfare knows, the retreat is probably the most dangerous part. This is where the Angels came in.

Soldiers are meant to have told colleagues and superiors that they saw angelic medieval archers armed with longbows protecting them against the advancing German army, although the angels have been described as many things over time.

In April of 1915, British Spiritualist Magazine published an article discussing these angelic and supernatural visions that appeared miraculously to save the retreating forces and enable them to escape to relative safety. Even reports of German soldiers with arrowhead shaped injuries were reported to add to the validity of the tale.

But did it really happen? Evidence would suggest not sadly, on the 29th September 1914, fantasy writer and journalist Arthur Machen published a short story called "The Bowmen" which he based on reports from the fighting at Mons but also included artistic license in the form of phantom bowmen from the Battle of Agincourt coming back to protect the commonwealth soldiers in the form of arrow wielding angels.

Even the Society for Psychical Research ran their own investigations into it and could not obtain any first hand testimonies back in 1915, leading them to conclude that the stories of supernormal forces were that of rumour and could not be given any genuine credence without genuine source.

What do I think? I think based on what I have read that on the balance of probability, it was a good story that was created from non fiction and embellished. Any good investigator or researcher needs to see evidence and whether that evidence is visual or from first hand testimony, none of that has been provided in relation to the Angels of Mons.

But ...we weren't there.....we don't know.....so maybe?

Heroes of History - Elizabeth Garrett
Written By Penny G Morgan

The 11th November 2018 marked the 100th anniversary of the end of the war that was meant to end all wars, The Great War, World War One. The focus on loss and sacrifice is quite rightly placed heavily on the soldiers who fought in those horrendous conditions – keep in mind, that on the first day of The Battle of the Somme, some 57,000 casualties were created from the allied forces alone – but what about the people who were dealing with the aftermath of man's need and lust for destruction? What about the women who were trying to pick up the pieces to keep this giant war machine rolling?

For that reason, I thought this new history blog should be focussed on one of those inspirational ladies who defied convention to do her bit and show what she was capable of to the men in charge.

Born into an already powerful family of women in the July of 1873, she was the daughter of some may say the first ever female medical doctor, Elizabeth Garrett Anderson and also the niece of one of the most well known leaders of the female suffrage movement, Millicent Fawcett.

Early in the outbreak of the First World War, her and her colleague and friend Flora Murray, approached the French Embassy with the idea of creating a hospital to treat the French victims of the fighting — knowing that the British government would dismiss their offer with an insignificant wave of the hand — and a short time after this, the Women's Hospital Corps was formed. Coupled with a cash injection due to fundraising efforts of £2,000, the Doctors found themselves in Paris, setting up their first hospital in the former Claridges Hotel.

A second French hospital was to follow before the British Government finally cottoned on to the professionalism and care that the Women's Hospital Corps offered and requested they establish a military hospital back in the UK, in the former St Giles Workhouse in Covent Garden. What is interesting is that despite the huge disparity in pay for many of the women seconded into the more traditional male roles during the war – women took home around 1/3rd of that of their male colleagues – Flora and Louisa were given the same remuneration as their male equivalents and also given military rank, Lieutenant Colonel and Major respectively.

This hospital was staffed entirely by women including doctors, surgeons, ophthalmic surgeons, dental surgeons, an anaesthetist, bacteriological and pathological experts and seven assistant doctors and surgeons, together with a full staff of women assistants. The records state that in the four years that they operated this endeavour, from March 1915 to October 1919, they treated in the region of 24,000 soldiers on an in patient basis and nearly the same number on an outpatient regime.

Pretty amazing when you think that the powers that be didn't believe women could be medical practitioners or in positions of authority, yet the care that was given by the Womens Hospital Corp induced a real sense of loyalty amongst those it treated, a comment home by one Australian Private illustrates this perfectly –

"The management is good, and the surgeons take great interest in and pains with their patients. They will persevere for months with a shattered limb before amputation, to try to save it...The whole hospital is a triumph for women, and incidentally it is a triumph for suffragette".

We will be looking at more women intrinsic to this time period over 2019, but do read more about the wonder Women's Hospital Corps and the advances that these women made in the attitude towards women by the greater public in the early part of the

20th century as I can only touch on their achievements in 500 or so words

If you want to listen to a show that I did with the wonderful Kerry Greenaway on World War One, click here   - https://www.spreaker.com/user/parasearchuk/the-sp irit-dimension-remembrance

Or via you tube - https://www.youtube.com/watch?v=bvoAN236nWU& index=30&list=UU9ti2d54cNbixWDWxmtIoBg

Who decides what history stays?
Written By Penny G Morgan

I am only going to warn you about this, but I have my soapbox out right now and I intend to stand on it and shout for the world to hear.....

Who are we to determine what pieces of history should stay? You hear stories of communist countries and heavily autocratic regimes doctoring the events of the past so as to write out anything that isn't to their liking – or to their ideology of ruling – but are we in the UK doing something similar?

I fear we are.

What do I mean by this? Well, take the less palatable historical events over the last 150 years or so, the increased use of the asylum, the workhouse movement, the world wars ...and you may realise to what I am alluding.

Let's look at a favourite subject of mine first, the workhouse movement. I would guess that a lot of people picture a poor sweet Oliver Twist type character gingerly asking for more gruel and the cruel Mr Bumble knocking him down? Just because Dickens wrote the character this way, doesn't mean that the workhouse was closely linked to hell, Dickens was a social critic so many of his works were designed to raise questions. The Workhouse was meant to be the place of last resort for the poor, and whilst the conditions inside weren't akin to a 5 star hotel, most provided food and shelter in return for labour. Whilst many critics of the Poor Laws saw this as nothing more than a factory using slave labour, for a lot, it probably saved their lives as with no welfare state to fall back on, what was their choice?

Why am I pointing this out? Can you name a workhouse that you can visit? I can think of three ...in the whole of England. Yes, there are many places that put on temporary exhibits, but I can think of three that are full time museums dedicated to the workhouse and the impact of life inside of one. Keep in mind that there were around 43 Poor Unions in England, and each of those would have sub unions where a home would be located, Essex for example had 22. So keep in mind each of these sub unions would have had a building allocated as a workhouse and you imagine the sheer enormity of it. Now, where was your local workhouse? Do you know?

This is my point, and if you are interested in this, have a listen to the Haunted Histories show that we put together called Ghosts of the Workhouse with Stuart and Rosey Dawson of Simply Ghost nights.

https://www.spreaker.com/user/parasearchuk/haunt
ed-histories-ghosts-of-the-workhous

Something so critical to our relatively recent past has been all but wiped out, these buildings – some requisitioned into hospitals, some converted into flats – are not being preserved for what they were as it's seen as being non PC history.

The same is happening with the old asylums, because of mental health treatment still being in its relative infancy, we look at the Victorian methods of treatment with horror. But who is to say that in 100 years time, our descendants will look at how we treat mental health issues and think our attitudes towards it are worthy of a raised eyebrow or two? . If you study the asylum movement in the Victorian era, it was innovative and would have helped people, yes, some people may have suffered but isn't that always the way with medical advancement?

Again, these buildings are being torn down or left to rot as nobody seems to want to admit that they had a purpose and are part of our history.

Which brings me to the last point, on the Essex Hertfordshire borders at present, a small (but growing) group of supporters are trying to stop a large developer ripping down POW Camp 116 to build 40 luxury homes – albeit that 25% of them are meant to be affordable, we shall see – whether the general public wants to believe that only the Germans and the Japanese had prisoner of war camps it is up to them, but we had them too. Whilst the buildings are in need of some very desperate TLC, there is no reason why it could not be opened as the southern version of Eden Camp – a brilliant museum in North Yorkshire – but they are on private land, and the owners have already decided to sell their soul. It probably doesn't help that the developers have already called it "a blotch (sic) on the landscape", think they mean a blotch in their bank account but who knows.

So what is my point? Well, we seem to cherish 1000 year old castles where people were thrown onto spikes in oubliettes and had their ligaments ripped apart on the rack, were beheaded simply for looking at a king the wrong way or having rats eat your intestines – but this is history which happened so long ago, nobody worries. But when it comes to more "Modern" history, we seem to view it with today's eyes and find it unpalatable, so don't want to preserve it, I for one, find this sad.

History rocks ...keep investigating!

Heroes of History - The She Wolf of France
Written By Penny G Morgan

One of the most interesting aspects of doing a show like Haunted Histories is the diverse range of events and periods in history that I have to study and explore to bring you - what I hope! – is an interesting show each week that doesn't just focus on the same era time and time again. Whilst I am very comfortable talking about all things Workhouse related, or all things World War related, looking at different events that I have to study from scratch gives me a chance to really flex my knowledge muscles and also learn about people that I had previously had serious misconceptions about.

What I thought I would do is highlight some of these in a series I am calling Heroes of History in the hope that

I can wet your appetite to broaden your horizons and opinions to about some of these characters.

Deal?

I am going to start with a lady who I believe, had she been alive now or even fifty years ago, would have probably either been running a multi million pound company or even been a fearless and effective world leader, Queen Isabella of France.

As with many royals of the day, we are talking 1295AD here, she was betrothed to another royal at a young age, in fact, her father King Philip IV of France, started discussing her marriage when Isabella was around 3 years old. She came to England at the age of 12 and married Edward II in 1308, a marriage which would last until his death in 1327, but more of that shortly.

Edward, although a reportedly handsome man who some historians believe was very in love with his wife, was given to forming very close relationships with specific male "friends" and this was something that gave Isabella cause for concern, Edward being more keen to do the more feminine pursuits of the time, and Isabella being more suited to working in a diplomat role and enjoying horse riding and hunting with dogs - a hobby which perhaps gave rise to her rather unflattering nickname of the She Wolf of France as she is meant to have favoured Irish Wolfhounds as her dog of choice.

She was accused of causing her husband's death and was even cited as a murderess by some, all because of her ability as a leader and her knack as a negotiator which saw her end the wars with Scotland, although, it has to be said that the nobility were not happy with her achievements as she used "feigns shock and horror" negotiation to end the years of war with our northern neighbours as opposed to beating the fight out of them.

When she was deposed, ironically by her son, Edward III, many history reports like to believe she was imprisoned in Castle Rising in Norfolk, but this is not the case. She lived a lavish lifestyle in her home, grew close to her daughter and grandson, frequently travelling around England. She was appointed to negotiate with France in 1348 and in 1358, was involved in the negotiations with Charles II of Navarre. Hardly the actions of someone under house arrest or worse, forced imprisonment by her son.

As notable figures in history go, it surprises me that not more people are aware of this amazing lady and that more Paranormal investigations do not mention her.

Have a listen to the show I did with the wonderful Viv Powell about her thoughts on Isabella and also her possible encounters with this amazing lady and see too, if you agree that she should be classed as a historical hero.

https://www.spreaker.com/user/parasearchuk/haunted-histories-castle-rising

Heroes of history - Hidden champions of Chernobyl
Written By Penny G Morgan

I would guess that you may be surprised that I have written an article relating to the events surrounding Chernobyl when I have only just done a show on the subject on Haunted Histories? But this subject matter has moved me to the extent that I feel that these men's names needed to become better known – even if that is only to those who read this blog.

Most people have heard of Chernobyl as its effects were wide reaching and caused ripples in areas further afield than just Europe. Pripyat is a place that urban explorers long to reconnoitre, its legend as a nuclear ghost town and one that is frozen in time with its Ferris wheel, dodgem cars and abandoned swimming pool all iconic images ingrained in human consciousness.

My show with Beth Darlington did touch on the events which led up to possibly the worst nuclear disaster in living history, but nobody mentions the men (and women) who were prepared to sacrifice themselves for the greater good. The Roof rats – as they were known – who went up to the destroyed reactor 4's roof to sweep in the radioactive material into the gaping hole ready for the giant sarcophagus to be placed over it – those roof rats were doing something that even the most ingenious robotic devices could not and were absorbing levels of radioactivity that would cause terminal radiation poisoning with 5 minutes or less. The reactor workers who stayed on straight after the explosion despite knowing they were taking on board killer levels of radiation. The Firefighters who again, didn't consider their own safety but merely wanting to stop anything worse happening. The Doctor who rushed over from the hospital at Pripyat to help those who had already started to show the horrific symptoms of radiation poisoning.

That's only a few of them, there were hundreds of thousands who risked their lives but there are three, who possibly saved Europe from nuclear disaster and rendering the whole continent uninhabitable.

Ten days after the initial explosion, the powers that be realised that the water cooling system had failed and a pool of water was amassing underneath the reactor. The concern was that a substance known as Corium – imagine radioactive lava - had formed from the melting graphite, nuclear fuel and molten concrete and was seeping through to this body of water. The only solution was to drain the pools as if the lava did drop into them, it could cause a resulting nuclear explosion of 3 to 5 megatons – Hiroshima was around 15 kilotons – to do this, somebody had to go into a pitch black badly damaged basement beneath a molten reactor core that was burning down towards them to manually turn the valves.

This job fell down to Alexei Ananenko, Valeri Bezpalov and Boris Baranov and the three men achieved their goal, they opened the valve, which drained the water and managed to avert a nuclear disaster of potentially cataclysmic proportions.

It's always been believed that the three brave men died a few weeks after from severe radiation poisoning, a fact which most would not be surprised about considering how

close they were to the leaking reactor and the fact they spent some time wading through radioactive water. However, a book by Andrew Leatherbarrow called "1:23:40 The incredible true story of the Chernobyl nuclear disaster" proves this to be false, instead finding that Ananenko was still alive and working in the nuclear industry, Bezpalov still alive and Baranov only having passed away in 2005 from a heart attack.

Now if any of you are nuclear physicists, nuclear engineers or any type of nuclear fission expert I apologise for any scientific errors, the purpose of this was to highlight the suicidal missions that many of those went on to save us from annihilation and their complete lack of attention seeking after the event, so much so that they were happy for the general public to believe they had perished to enable them to carry on with their lives.

Brave men indeed, but it makes me wonder why their names aren't more well known? Is it because of the secrecy surrounding the former Soviet Union? Is it that people have forgotten about Chernobyl? Or is it because these brave souls were never part of a reality TV show like Big Love Jungle Island or something that nobody really cares?

Well I care, and I thank them with all of my being for the sacrifice they were willing to make to save the world.

Heroes of History – The Film Star Inventor
Written By Penny G Morgan

It is a common misapprehension that an individual cannot be beautiful and possess above average intelligence, this is a view that many had of one of the most aesthetically pleasing actresses of her day, Hedy Lamarr.

Lamarr was born in Vienna, Austria on the 9th November 1914, at the age of 12 she won a beauty contest in her home town and perhaps that established her career as being a pretty face and nothing more. After taking acting lessons, she started appearing in films in her native Austria, one of her most notorious roles having been as the neglected younger wife of an older man in the movie "Ecstasy". The title is certainly not a misnomer as this picture became infamous due to her having simulated an orgasm on screen and also numerous close up nude and partially clothed scenes – which incidentally, she said afterwards were not of her own volition and that she had been tricked by the director, Gustav Machaty.

At the age of 18 she entered her first marriage -there were to be six in total – with the arms dealer, Friedrich Mandl, 15 years her senior. This was not a union that her Jewish descendent parents were particularly enamoured of due to Mandl's links with not only Mussolini, but also the Nazi regime and Hitler in particular. Whilst this marriage was not to last and he is reported to have kept Hedy a prisoner, it did introduce her to science as she was privy to the meetings and consultations that Mandl had with his weapons developers.

Fast forward to the outbreak of World War 2 and Lamarr was in the United States and working as an actress for MGM – having been scouted in London after her escape from Vienna – and whilst her application to join the National Inventors Council was turned down ("your fame is better used to sell war bonds little lady" ok, so I'm paraphrasing there but you get my drift), it didn't stop this amazing woman inventing. One of the men that she dated in-between husbands was the aviation hero Howard Hughes, and it was in fact he who recognised Lamarr's gift for inventing and put his entire team of scientists and engineers at her disposal after she presented him with a sketch of a much faster aircraft by creating a hybrid of the fastest fish and the fastest bird.

It was during WW2, and in 1942 that Hedy heard of the problems facing the US Navy with regard to their torpedoes and the Axis forces managing to jam the radio signal that controlled their trajectory. She contacted her friend, George Antheil, and between them they came up with an invention that is known as frequency hopping or "spread Spectrum", which enabled the radio signal to jump around frequencies and to stop the possibility of it being jammed. On the 11th August 1942 they were granted US Patent 2,292,387 and decided to give it to the US military for use against the enemy. Whether it was Lamarr's beauty, the fact she was a woman or just the fact that the US military did not accept help from outside sources, they did not use it, but waited over 20 years before the concept was rediscovered and utilised during the Cuban Missile Crisis.

This meant that Hedy (and George for that matter) did not ever receive a cent in payment for their idea and even more shocking, did not receive any recognition until more than fifty years later – by which time Hedy was an elderly recluse and unable to

capitalise upon her genius. The invention of frequency hopping is what enables us to have things like Wi-Fi, GPS and Bluetooth today, so without the questioning mind of Hedy Lamarr, we would be both tied by cables and lost.....

Heroes of History – No job for a woman
Written By Penny G Morgan

Being an avid reader of everything fiction and non-fiction, it is hardly surprising that every so often I come across names that connect the dots and make me want to learn more about their particular contribution to history.

I've just finished a book about the Spanish Civil War and in it, two names that should ring bells with anyone with a basic general knowledge were mentioned, Ernest Hemingway and his then mistress, Martha Gellhorn.

You can probably tell by the title of this piece that it isn't Hemingway that I plan to focus on; its Martha and how possibly she changed the face of war journalism for women – and perhaps men too.

The Spanish Civil war deserves many articles in it's own right, the acts of atrocity perpetuated -predominantly, it has to be said by Franco's Nationalist side - are horrific and it was also the German testing ground for mass bombardment from the air to strike terror into civilians that was to be used to such horrific effect a mere three years later during World War II, but more of that in future blogs. My focus is on Martha, and how she paved the way for future female war correspondents such as Kate Adie and the late Marie Colvin.

I can't in a blog of only 600 words or so go into all of Gellhorn's literary work, one look at her bibliography would tell you what a prolific writer she was, but I do want to focus on one of the tales that surrounds her and why I think she is worthy of the title as that of a hero of history.

Born in St Louis, Missouri in 1908, it can only be assumed that the influence of a suffragist mother implanted with a strong sense of self belief in her and the drive to compete in a man's world. It was some years later, in Key West Florida that at the age of 28 on a family holiday, she was to meet a huge influence on her life, Ernest Hemingway and be persuaded to go out to Spain to cover the Civil War which was tearing apart the country and its people. It was her inclusion in an event which has its 75th anniversary on 6th June 2019 that she was best known for.

For Martha was going to be the only woman present at the Normandy Beach Invasion, better known as the D Day landings.

By 1944, she and Hemingway had been married for four years; however, as was perhaps inevitable between two such independent and driven characters, that which had attracted them to each other was also going to tear them apart. It is reported that by this time, her husband had already started to tire of her mission to be reporting on war around the world rather than playing the dutiful wife and warming his bed. In a move perhaps synonymous with the somewhat egotistical and narcissistic reputation of Hemingway, he had press permission to be on the beaches on 6th June 1944 and she did not. It is reported in various media that he chose the somewhat more secure confines of a military ship and Gellhorn was to masquerade as a stretcher bearer to enable her to be in the thick of the destruction. She wrote for her article in Collier's Weekly (who her now estranged husband had gone to and obtained that invaluable press pass, although she was the more respected journalist it must be said)

"It was no fun at all, considering the mines and obstacles that remained in the water, the sunken tanks with only their radio antennae showing above water, the drowned bodies that still floated past."

It is possible that it was Gellhorn's happy consent to be seen as one of the boys that made her so readily accepted by the troops that she shared both a laugh and a conversation with, the fact that she refused to be told no and was determined to cover these battles from her point of view, a point of view not highlighting the actual weapons or the power of this warfare, but the social aspect, the effect on humanity that has made her so important and so critical to writers going forwards.

But I will leave you with these words written by the lady herself.

"I didn't write, I just wandered about"

Please listen to more history content on my podcast, Haunted Histories, every Wednesday at 9pm on Parasearch Radio.

It's all in a number.
Written By Penny G Morgan

When you ask someone to name pioneers of computing, they are most likely to mention historical greats such as Alan Turing, maybe Bill Gates or the late Steve Jobs, but I doubt many would think of a woman who was actually the daughter of one of the most infamous Casanova poets of the early 19th century.

Augusta Ada was born to Lord and Lady Annabella Byron in December 1815 and only five weeks after her birth, both she and her mother were to leave Byron and to live at Ada's matrimonial grandparents. Even as a newborn, Ada was to be a victim of the cult of celebrity. We may think of treating stars as nothing short of deities as being a modern late 20th century invention, especially with every other person appearing in magazines and on television these days not appearing to have any discernible talent other than having caused some kind of stir on the glut of reality shows that permeate our screens, but many researchers into the life of Byron would disagree. The reason that Annabella left with a new born was in part, due to the scandal that was starting to gain credence, along with her husbands deteriorating mental state, he had been having an illicit affair with his half sister Augusta Leigh – a dalliance which was to produce a daughter, Medora. The whispers and attack on the Byron name were enough to force the Lord himself to leave the country and to never see his daughter Ada again.

Ada was not a healthy child, a bout of measles had left her temporarily paralysed but this did not stop her interest in maths and science, at the age of 12 for example, young Ada decided she wanted to fly so began to methodically research materials for wings and even conducted meticulous studies of birds to ascertain the correct ratio of wing to body. Fast forward to Miss Byron aged 17, and an affair and attempted elopement with her then tutor raises the question, had she inherited her father's "lust for life" per se as it could not have been said to have resulted from nurture as she had been without contact from five weeks old.

It was shortly after this that she was introduced to the polymath Charles Babbage, a relationship of mutual respect and learning that was perhaps unusual for the time. Married in 1835, and 3 children followed over the next four years, many would think that the newly named Ada Lovelace – not the name of a porn star which was the answer given on a quiz show I was watching once – may have started to calm down and embrace her new life, alas this was not the case. Scandals and rumours of extra marital affairs were to follow Ada much the same way as they had her father, but you can surmise from her lack of denial and her somewhat open acceptance of that side of life that these were more fact than fiction.

Unfortunately it is much of this that still lingers around Ada like a malodorous scent rather than her work with Babbage on his Analytical Machine, widely believed to be the forerunner to the modern computer. During a lecture given by Babbage in Turin, a young Italian Scientist Luigi Menabrea compiled an article, written in French, which Ada was asked to transcribe, an undertaking she took on and completed with additional notes, more than doubling the original piece. She had devised an algorithm that would incorporate coding for the engine to be able to use letters and symbols as well as the typical numbers. Another theory she put forward in this piece was that of instruction repetition, known now in computer science as looping.

Whilst her achievements were not recognised to the extent they should have been during her lifetime, it took another hundred years after her death at the age of 36 (exactly the same age as her father incidentally) for her research to be rediscovered and given the plaudits it deserves.

Was Ada her father's daughter? I think very much so, not just with her love of excess – be it gambling or lust – but also her genius, with intelligence coming from both sides of her gene pool, her love of maths and the possession of knowledge can easily be attributed to her mother who was a well known and incredibly well educated philanthropist.

Like a lot of female pioneers, who knows what she could have achieved given the right encouragement, we will never know, but she certainly deserves to be remembered as a hero of history

Have a listen to the podcast I did with Barrie John about Ada's former ancestral home, Newstead Abbey.

https://www.spreaker.com/user/parasearchuk/haunted-histories-a-return-to-newstead-w

"Frankly my Dear, I don't give a damn."
Written By Penny G Morgan

Those little words uttered by a moustached southern gentleman from the film Gone with the Wind can only belong to one person, the actor who played the roguish socialite Rhett Butler, the quintessential gentleman Clark Gable.

But how many of you know about the man behind the character? Who could tell me what tragedy befell him that caused the man who Hitler himself is supposed to have cited as one of his favourite actors (and subsequently offered a reward to anyone who could catch him unscathed).

Born in February 1901 in the US state of Ohio, it took him until the age of 29 before he started being offered leading man role in the film industry, and it was in 1939 that one of his best known films was released, the fabled Gone with the Wind. It was also the year that he was to marry his third wife, seven years his junior, the actress Carole Lombard. Some say that this period was the happiest that Gable had ever been, but sadly, this period of elation was to only last three years, because in January 1942, whilst returning from a War bond promotion tour, Lombard's aircraft was to crash killing all onboard – including fifteen servicemen who were on their way to California for training.

Following being Widowed, Gable decided to do his part for the war effort and joined the United States Army Air Force, unlike his fellow movie star the wonderful Jimmy Stewart, he was not a pilot but an enlisted gunner and despite the protests of the MGM film studio (assets were to be protected, MGM did something very similar with Stewart) he went to train as an observer/gunner with the 351st Bombardment Group (Heavy) and within a short time was shipped out to RAF Polebrook in early 1943 to work as a photographer and aerial gunner on board B-17 Flying Fortresses.

Whilst his official log states he flew five missions during 1943, I have found the reports of four, but many veterans remember him going up many more times – based on what I know about the flying in WW2, five would seem a very low number. However, it could be said that his late wife was looking down on him and protecting him as a mission on 12th August 1943 to bomb a steel works in Bochum Germany could have ended his life. Deciding that he

wanted a better view than the Waist Gunner position afforded, he wedged himself in behind the top turret position. The mission log (which you can access if you so choose, may I recommend the website dedicated to these brave men and women, www.351st.org) states that the level of flak was incredibly high and powerful, but it was only upon landing that Gable realised that a 20mm shell had burst through the flight deck, and exited unexploded a mere 30 cm from his head, although it had taken out the heel of his boot. I did do a bit of a search on that particular aircraft 42-29863 and it managed to fly 80 missions before it was shot down in February 1944 under pilot Captain Carson, ironically, that was also his 80th mission according to the record logs, you can never assume that all crew flew the same aircraft each time, especially as Carson alternated between pilot and co pilot.

Gable returned to the US in November 1943 to finish editing his film and whilst his commission remained active until 26th September 1947, he never flew in combat again.

He was to marry a further two times, before dying from a cardiac event in 1960 at the age of 59 and whilst it was common knowledge in Hollywood that he had fathered an illegitimate child with actress Loretta Young many years previously, he was never to be a parent to her or to meet his son John, who was born four months after his death.

Although I will close this blog with this Gable quote, seeing as I opened it with one

"Honey, we all got to go sometime, reason or no reason. Dying is as natural as living. The man who's too afraid to die is too afraid to live.

Coombe Abbey
Written By Penny G Morgan

When I was asked to write a piece about Coombe Abbey I did wonder where to start, the building is not "obvious" from the road, in fact, when I headed over there in November 2018 to represent Parasearch at Sage Paracon I actually thought my Sat nav was on the blink when it told me to turn right down this long winding driveway, then the Abbey comes into view.

I had been up from around 5am that day to ensure I got to the venue on time and was not to be disappointed by the grandeur of the place, a somewhat involuntary sound of "wow" came out of my mouth more than once and I did go for a little wander around the grounds before going in to introduce myself to the Sage organiser, MJ Dickson.

What is now a hotel is truly stunning, and the structure does seem to watch and follow you as you walk around, but why? What is its history? What has it seen?

There are plenty of "ghost" stories associated with the Abbey, the mistreated stable girl who put a curse on the family living there, a horseman who is seen near the old coach house and a Victorian woman riding a bicycle nearby.

If you're fortunate enough to have a ticket for Sage Paracon, and 2019 is going to be no different, you get to investigate parts of the hotel with some of the special guests, but what past events are there to dig into?

A cursory glance online produced such a real bevy of information that I could probably write a whole series of articles regarding this location so please do not treat the information that I am about to come out with as being all there is.

Perhaps unsurprisingly – the clue is in the name! –the site was originally an abbey, but not just any old abbey, it was probably the most powerful and rich monastery in Warwickshire. Even though you would think the combination of peaceful prayer, the giving of alms to the poor and having land and property donated to them by locals wishing to get into Gods good graces would have made for a peaceful existence it did not however, stop the murder of the Abbot Geoffrey in 1345, an act so heinous that the then King, Edward III ordered 6 justices to investigate. There is a strongly held belief that the spectral monk who is meant to cause chaos in the now hotel kitchens and be seen walking the grounds, is poor slain Geoffrey, although who knows for sure?

In 1470, King Edward IV stayed at Coombe, under the hospitality of the Ciscertian monks and Abbott Alexander whilst travelling to Coventry to do battle with his former friend, Richard Neville the Earl of

Warwick, aka, The Kingmaker – and we all know how that turned out. The Wars of the Roses are so complicated it is no wonder that historians study it indefinitely to put all the pieces together.

Jump forward a further 150 years or so, and the reformation has been and gone, the crown has seized the monasteries and religious Papal houses and passed them over to in favour nobles for development into country homes. Coombe was then owned by one Sir John Harrington, a Scottish descendant who could trace his lineage to Robert Bruce and used this to become part of King James inner circle. So much so, that when the King needed a guardian for his daughter, Princess Elizabeth (later to become Elizabeth of Bohemia) and she went to live at Coombe in around 1603.

Those bright sparks (you will get the joke in a minute) in you may also know what was brewing around this time, Guy Fawkes and his band of men were planning the Gunpowder Plot, conniving to murder King James and place Elizabeth (as a Catholic puppet) on the throne. To enable their plan to work, they schemed to kidnap the young princess and in order to cause a distraction, timed it with Lord Harrington leaving the 9 year old little girl unsupervised whilst he wants on a hunting trip. Unfortunately for the conspirators, Harrington got wind of their machinations and sent Elizabeth safely to Coventry, the schemers were either killed or caught and sent to London for questioning and execution.

The house then passed into the Craven family whose descendants were to live on the estate until 1921 when it was sold onto a builder and then subsequently sold to the local authority.

There are many deaths mentioned (due to old age) in relation to the abbey in the newspapers during the period 1940 to around 1980, but one is incredibly sad, and that was on 15th November 1978 when walkers discovered a woman who had burnt herself to death along the driveway leading to the abbey. Whilst it was subsequently determined (after she was identified) that she had been suffering from severe depression, the newspapers also pointed out that she was the second woman to take her own life by fire in a mere 3 days, a 42yr old mother of six had seemingly committed suicide the same way on Hearsall Common in Coventry.

Maybe I watch too many shows like Mindhunter and Criminal Minds, but that seems very coincidental to me.

So Coombe Abbey has something for everyone, stunning architecture, beautiful grounds, an amazingly rich history, a reception area which I guarantee will blow your mind and if you are available between 7th and 10th November 2019, check out http://www.sageparacon.co.uk/ and treat yourself to something very special whilst you're there.

But between you and me ...I plan to take my husband there sometime, but please do not mention any of these or I doubt I will be able to get him to get out of the car.

Heroes of History - Desmond Doss
Written By Penny G Morgan

Can you imagine walking into a terrifying warzone, going into the very thick of the fighting and be totally weapon less......and not just devoid of any type of firearm, but have that kind of vulnerability by choice?

That was the decision that a young man from Lynchburg, Virginia made when he enlisted into the military during World War Two, his name was Desmond Doss. He was born in February 1919 and raised as a strict Seventh Day Adventist by his mother, with a strong belief system that promoted a vegetarian lifestyle, the keeping of the Sabbath and strict non-violence. Once he finished his education he began work as a shipbuilder and this alone would have given him a valid reason to not enlist but he chose to go to war and signed up on 1st April 1942.

I first found out about this individual when I watched a Mel Gibson film called "Hacksaw Ridge", now, I have to be honest here, my incentive to watch the film was not actually the history side of it but more to do with one of the actors appearing but nevertheless, it introduced me to the amazing story of Desmond Doss – of which only a small portion is covered.

So, here we have this man who is basically a conscientious objector, who argued that he would not take up arms against the "enemy" but wanted to do his part for his country as a medic. He would refuse to train on the sabbath, was bullied and beaten up by many of his fellow recruits yet he still found himself in April of 1945, climbing up cargo netting tagged onto 400 foot jagged cliffs into one of the bloodiest battles of the pacific with an estimated 160,000 casualties on both sides. The relentless fighting went on for nearly a month and Doss was right there, treating the injured, frequently under heavy enemy fire whilst he dragged or carried them to safety.

It was what he did about a week into the assault that our unlikely hero found himself the only medic still remaining as his unit drove forward in the attempt to take the ridge from the Japanese. Under incredibly heavy artillery shelling, the U.S. forces were driven back down leaving Doss on his own. Through the night he tended to the injured and dying, one by one he would drag each one to the edge of the cliff and lower them in a rope harness he had made. He is estimated to have rescued over 75 men that night, although the ever-humble Doss always said he believed it was less than 50, and in fact, some Army records state it was nearer 100. Whatever the truth, he worked tirelessly and at great risk to himself to save as many men as possible. It is during his ceaseless sacrifice that he is said to have uttered the phrase "Dear God, just let me get one more man".

That was not to be the end of his heroics however, days later he was injured in the leg by a grenade and rather than use up the scant supply of medics by calling for help, he treated himself and waited five hours to be rescued. It was whilst being taken to safety – after refusing to be carried on a stretcher and giving it to a soldier he deemed with worse injuries – he was shot in the arm and this fractured his arm which was never the same again.

You may think that a leg injury and a shattered limb was enough, but no, whilst being treated in a tropical hospital he was to contract Tuberculosis which resulted in his losing a lung and 5 ribs.

But Desmond was to be awarded something that never before had been given to a person who had refused to bear arms in the war, the Medal of Honour. To be even more detail orientated, he was also awarded a Purple Heart and a Bronze Star, all without killing another man. Whilst some called him a coward for refusing to raise a gun, his former commanding officer Captain Jack Glover said

"He was one of the bravest people alive, and then to have him end up saving my life was the irony of the whole thing," especially as Glover was one of the senior officers who had tried to get Doss thrown out on multiple occasions.

Desmond survived the war, survived having tuberculosis and even survived deafness in 1976 due to an overdose of antibiotics, but he passed away at the age of 87 in 2006 without knowing the amount of people who are now familiar with his amazing heroism in the face of total and utter chaos.

The Canary sings....
Written By Penny G Morgan

With this year's Remembrance Sunday fast approaching, I wanted to write a history blog that would pay homage to all of those who have given their lives and made sacrifices in order for the majority of us to be kept safe. I have put together many accounts of people who have shown, what I believe to be, dedication over and above that which is expected, but this is to be slightly different.

When you mention the First World War, what comes to mind? Probably trenches, the Somme and maybe airship raids? Whilst all of those are very valid and necessary thoughts, I like to look at the social impact and primarily, how it affected the fairer sex left behind. It is not uncommon to think that women did not play a huge role until the Second World War some twenty five years after the start of the Great War, but this is not true. Many women were putting themselves in harm's way, albeit not being fired upon by any enemy combatant.

I am alluding to the munitions workers, the too often ignored backbone of the home front effort.

In the summer of 1914, nobody envisaged the great toll that the fighting would have on both sides of the war, and by 1915, there was a shortage of shells being produced – for the purposes of this piece I am focussing on the British side – so much so, that there are reports that only four shells a day were being fired to try and eke out the fast dwindling supply. It was due to this that the future Prime Minister, David Lloyd George became the Minister of Munitions and set about building hundreds of thousands of munition works – producing TNT, making the shells and all the other requirements of a huge war machine. It is reckoned that by the summer of 1918, there were over 200,000 different factories with workers exceeding the millions operating them. Many of these workers were female who had come from a more blue collar background and had formerly been in domestic service.

It was incredibly dangerous work, the buildings were known as Danger Sheds and being found to have something as trivial as a metal hair pin in your pocket could give rise to a docking of pay, sacking or even worse, prison. Materials like Trinitrotoluene (TNT to you and I) was notoriously toxic, so much so, that the women who worked with it had their skin turn yellow and were likened to Canaries. The reports of the workers who died from TNT poisoning are scarce, but it is believed to have been in the hundreds. Deaths from inhalation or absorption of chemicals was not the only risk – think of the different types of shells used in war, and they estimate that the British fired at least 170million during those four years of battle – the equipment that was used to handle these incredibly volatile materials was archaic and was the cause of many accidents, nearly all had fatalities.

Take the story of Mabel Lethbridge, at 17 she lied about her age to work at the shell filling factory in Hayes Middlesex, operating machinery to put the highly explosive Amatol into the weapons. On the 23rd October 1917, an accident involving her role and the inadequacy of the tools that the workers were given gave rise to a huge explosion. Mabel lost a leg, broke her arm and suffered a multitude of other severe injuries, but due to the fact that she was under 18 and had lied about her age, she did

not receive a pension, in fact, the factory commission even tried to convince the public that it was her being under 18 that caused the machine to malfunction.

A cursory glance at the newspapers from that period shows how vast this problem of accidents were, in just over one month in 1917, there are a myriad of articles relating to explosions in munitions factories and the resulting deaths, and that is assuming that all deaths were recorded. We may we think illegal immigrants and undocumented workers are a 21st century issue they most certainly are not. Factor in as well that 80% of those employed were women and you can see the issue here.

So, the point of this brief article is not to cast a shadow on the female staff, it is not to criticise the bosses working them to the bone with 12 hour plus shifts with very little support it is not even to lambast the pathetic arguments that were used to avoid paying out pensions to a young woman injured in the line of duty. The purpose is this, when you wear your poppy on Remembrance Sunday, remember those people who may not have been fighting front line in the mud and rats, remember those people that without their own personal sacrifices and willingness to face disability or even death every time they went to work, there would have been nothing to fight with, please remember the munitions workers.

"The guns out there are roaring fast, the bullets fly like rain; The aeroplanes are curvetting, they go and come again; The bombs talk loud; the mines crash out; no trench their might withstands. Who helped them all to do their job? The girls with yellow hands."

Untold tragedies
Written by Penny G Morgan

Just recently, I was listening to my Parasearch colleague Kerry talk in her live Monday broadcast about how history is written by the winners, and it led me to thinking about the propaganda and false facts that are spread continuously to either assuage an individual's guilt or to make a situation appear more palatable.

Whilst researching for a short presentation I was putting together for a local primary school on World War II, I came across a story that I had a vague recollection of from past reading, but when I dug further into it, the result left me shocked at the potential misinformation that had been spread.

That being what happened at South Hallsville School in Canning Town, in September 1940

I would guess that the main events of 1940 that spring to mind – in the dim dark recesses of childhood history classes – are most likely the Battle of Britain (official dates being 10th July 1940 to 31st October 1940) and Operation Dynamo, aka the evacuation of Dunkirk (26th May 1940 to 4th June 1940), the bombing of a part of East London probably not even registering as being that important in the grand scheme of things.

I disagree, I think what happened on the 10th of September in the E16 area of London was not only about to change how citizens protected themselves in the event of an air raid but also to make them realise that perhaps the Government was not their friend.

Many of the residents of this part of London had lost their dwellings due to the bombings that had been targeting the docks nearby and also the proliferation of industrial buildings. These people would live close by to their place of work, as did their extended families and so the destruction would mean that entire groups were rendered homeless. Without cousins or grandparents to go and lodge with, they had no choice but to place themselves on the list for evacuation to safer areas of the UK.

These local residents were told to take refuge in the local South Hallsville School which had a large basement whilst they waited for the buses to take them out of the city, however transport never arrived. It is said that those people sheltered there for three days, relatives only finding out later that the drivers of the vehicles had been sent to Camden Town and not Canning Town, in peacetime probably a mistake you would laugh at, but not for these poor souls. On that fateful day in September the school took a direct hit from a parachute bomb which caused the building to collapse into itself, the subterranean layer acting as a giant hole for the rubble to fall into.

The official records state that "only" 77 people died in this horrific incident, the Government did not want to release details of large civilian deaths as this would hamper the war effort and can do spirit that they were relying on, but people talk. The locals estimated that the death toll was much higher, nearer to 600 people they believe. The area was tarmacked over and a memorial placed there, but it did cause the powers that be to re-examine how they provided shelter to the general public who did not have access to private shelters and were not happy congregating in one building. Some historians believe that it was due to this incident that the underground

stations were opened up for those needing to get away from the melee of ordnance constantly raining down upon the city – but maybe it was also that they gave up trying to stop people breaking into them to try and preserve their lives?

Sadly this did not stop another of the worst civilian death tolls of the war taking place, but that is an article for another day. The point of this blog is do not always believe what official reports want you to hear, never stop asking questions.

Printed in Great Britain
by Amazon